695kw

Jill Turnbull. £2

Blue-Printed Earthenware
1800-1850

Books by the same author

Blue and White Transfer Ware 1780-1840
British Art Pottery
Buying Antiques Dictionary of Names
Collecting Bookmarkers
Don't Throw It Away
Historic English Inns

BLUE-PRINTED
EARTHENWARE 1800-1850

A. W. Coysh

David & Charles
Newton Abbot · *London* · *North Pomfret (Vt)*

First published 1972
Second impression 1980

0 7153 5796 4

Printed in Great Britain
by Redwood Burn Ltd Trowbridge & Esher
for David & Charles (Publishers) Limited
Brunel House Newton Abbot Devon

Published in the United States of America
by David & Charles Inc.
North Pomfret Vermont 05053 USA

CONTENTS

Acknowledgements   6

Purposeful Collecting   7

Conventions and References   9

Makers and Patterns 1800–1850   10

Problem Pieces   98

Small Wares   110

Index   112

ACKNOWLEDGEMENTS

My earlier book on *Blue and White Transfer Ware 1780-1840* published in 1970, led to a most fruitful correspondence with collectors all over Britain and in the USA. As a result I was able to see many patterns hitherto unrecorded and to assemble much new information. It seemed desirable that this materia! should be made generally available and a number of collectors have allowed me to use photographs of blue and white wares in their possession. For this facility I wish to thank Mrs Elizabeth Carter, Mr Richard Clements, Mr and Mrs D. A. Dalzell-Piper, Mr and Mrs J. G. Evans, Mr and Mrs J. K. des Fontaines, Mr B. G. Gough, Mr Robin Gurnett, Mrs W. E. Haighton, Mrs V. Heap, Mr Ian Hendeson, Mr and Mrs S. Henrywood, Mrs R. Holloway, Mrs Jean Latham, Mrs D. Pugh, Mr and Mrs Martin Pulver, Mrs P. F. Trethowan and the Wellcome Institute Trustees. Specific acknowledgements have been included in the captions. For information and useful discussion I am also grateful to Mr Timothy Clark, Mr A. E. Fields, Mr John D. Griffin, Mr John Higgins, Mr W. L. Little, Mr T. A. Lockett, Mr and Mrs John May, Mrs Jean Miller, Mr Colin Mures, The Rev Canon J. J. F. Scammell, Mr Hugh Stretton, Mrs Joan Whittock, Mr T. C. Wilkinson, Mrs N. Williams and Mr J. McCallum Young.

Finally, I owe once again a very special debt of gratitude to Mr Richard Clements not only for his fine photography but also for preparing a layout for the illustrations which has made it possible to face them with the relevant text.

A. W. Coysh

PURPOSEFUL COLLECTING

Few people fully appreciate the interest and aesthetic pleasure to be derived from collecting blue-printed earthenware. The field is very wide indeed for several hundred British potters produced literally thousands of different patterns in the first half of the nineteenth century. The enthusiastic beginner tends to think he should buy every piece he sees or can afford. Later, if he deserves the name of collector, he will become more selective. Some notes on possibilities may perhaps help to accelerate the process.

Apart from those who acquire blue-printed wares for their decorative value, there are many specialist collectors. The main spheres of interest are as follows:

1. Potteries and Marks

Interest in determining the provenance of blue-printed wares ranks high among collectors. For this reason pieces with impressed or printed marks, or both, are usually considered more desirable than those which are unmarked. Marks usually, though not invariably, reveal the name of the maker and often much other information—the locality of the pottery, the name of the pattern or series of patterns, occasionally even the date of manufacture or the name of the retailer. Some people like to collect the wares of a single firm—Brameld, Davenport, Leeds Old Pottery, Rogers or Spode. Others may study a group of factories—the Yorkshire potteries, for example, or those in the north-east of England close to the Tyne, Wear and Tees. In some cases there are books on individual potteries. Leonard Whiter's book on *Spode* and T. A. Lockett's book on *Davenport* are good examples. R. C. Bell's *Tyneside Potteries* and Oxley Grabham's *Yorkshire Potteries, Pots and Potters* first published in 1916 and recently reprinted, deal with pottery districts.

2. Chinoiserie Patterns

Blue-printing on earthenwares started in Britain in 1780 and until the first decade of the nineteenth century nearly all the patterns were derived from designs on imported Chinese porcelain. These were introduced in great variety and gradually became standardised in the popular willow pattern as we know it today. Collectors of these early wares are sometimes able to match them with the original Chinese designs from which they were derived. A paired collection would be of outstanding interest.

3. Topographical Patterns

Very many blue-printed wares carry patterns derived from illustrations in books of the period (or earlier), particularly those on architecture and travel. Series were produced with views of abbeys, castles, country houses and river scenery and many wares intended for export to America carry prints of American towns and cities, or of historical events. Many of the marks bear the name of the place (Plate 39), often without the name of the maker, and many collectors seek pieces with 'named views' (see pp 100-3). Sometimes they try to match the scene with that on a later postcard, or a modern photograph taken from the same view-point.

Foreign scenes are also common and discussion with a print collector will often lead to the identification of the actual print from which a pattern has been derived. Riley's *Eastern Street Scene Pattern*, for example, illustrated in *Blue and White Transfer Ware 1780-1840*, Plate 74, has now proved to have been derived from two engravings in T. and W. Daniell's *Oriental Scenery* published in 1797. It combines 'The Sacred Tree of the Nindoor at Gyah, Bahar' from Part 1, plate 15 with a 'A view of the Chitpore Road, Calcutta' from Part II, plate 3. Here is a vast field for research.

4. Botanical Patterns

A number of potters produced floral patterns of various kinds but the outstanding examples are from the Wedgwood Etruria Works (see pp 90-93). Many designs in the *Botanical Flowers Series* were copied or derived from contemporary botanical publications. A complete check list with the sources of the patterns could certainly be made but would probably take a devoted collector some years to complete.

5. Zoological Patterns

A collection could be made solely of patterns with identifiable birds and animals. Job Meigh produced a series called *Zoological Sketches* and animals or birds appear on the wares of Adams, Spode, Rogers and Stevenson, among others.

6. Commemorative and Historical Patterns

The finest historical blue prints are those on a series made by Jones & Son (see pp 40-1) and similar designs were often made to mark notable events such as the Battle of Trafalgar (p 109), The Eglinton Tournament, the Coronations of George IV and William IV, and the opening of the first railway. A fine collection of blue-printed wares with portraits of Nelson may be seen in the Nelson Museum, Priory Street, Monmouth.

7. *Literary Patterns*
Some wares carry prints derived from illustrations in books by well-known authors published in the first half of the nineteenth century such as Byron (pp 48-9), Dickens (p 65) and Sir Walter Scott (p 25).

8. *Rural Scenes*
Patterns with English country scenes abound and many of them reveal interesting facts about the costume, dwellings, implements and occupations of the country people of the period. These are the most typically 'English' of all Staffordshire blue-printed wares and provide appropriate decoration on country-made oak furniture.

9. *Medical Ceramics*
Many blue-printed wares were made for those engaged in the rearing of children and nursing of the sick—feeding bottles, pap boats, feeding cups and bordaloues. Any collector interested in this field should see the collection of the Wellcome Institute of the History of Medicine in the Wellcome Building, Euston Road, London, N.W.1.

Collection Records
All serious collectors are well advised to keep records either in card index or book form. Provided these are kept up-to-date this is not an onerous task. Once the date, place of purchase and purchase price of a piece have been noted, an accurate description should be entered. It is surprising how many details are seen when writing this up which would otherwise have escaped notice. A photograph is always a useful addition since it can be sent by post for other collectors to see. At this point the interesting detective work begins—who made it? When was it made? Who designed or engraved the pattern? From what source was this derived? It will seldom be possible to answer all these questions but much information is already available thanks to the researches of enthusiasts. The author has in his collection a Wedgwood comport with a fine botanical design (p 91). A surprising amount of information about this pattern has been culled from the detailed research by Mrs Una des Fontaines. One is able to record that it was produced during the period when John Wedgwood, F.H.S., F.L.S., was actively engaged in the management of the Wedgwood Etruria Works and that he almost certainly sketched out the design for the pattern himself and briefed the engraver when it was first produced. We know that the blue-printed version was engraved by John Robinson in 1809 and that it was launched commercially in 1811. We can name the flowers—the Starry water lily, the Sacred Lotus of Buddha and the Lotus of Egypt—and we know that these were copied or derived from the *Botanist's Repository* for October 1803 and the *Botanical Magazines* for December 1804 and February 1806.

This is just an example of the kind of information one always hopes to secure, though it is unusual to be able to trace the history of a piece in such detail.

At the other extreme one is faced with the problem of the unmarked piece about which there is no information at all. Whatever the problems, the detective work involved is always fascinating but is seldom fruitful unless the approach is scientific.

CONVENTIONS AND REFERENCES

In order to avoid misunderstanding the following conventions have been adopted in this book.

A maker is named only when the piece is clearly marked with the name of the firm or factory and there can be no doubt at all about its origin. Fortunately blue-printed earthenware is seldom, if ever, faked. The only examples known to the author are of some Dr Syntax patterns originally produced by Clews but the experienced collector will not, as a rule, be deceived by these. Modern reproductions are so poorly printed when compared with the early wares that confusion can hardly arise particularly as they are almost invariably marked 'England', a certain sign of modernity. Other terms must be defined more exactly.

'Attributed to'—followed by the name of the maker, means that the author has no doubt at all in his mind that the particular piece conforms in every way to known marked specimens by that maker with similar pattern, body and glaze.

'Probably'—followed by the name of the maker, means that all the available evidence points to the fact that the wares were made by the maker named but that some doubt exists.

'Possibly'—followed by the name of the maker, means that some characteristic of the wares suggests the particular maker but that the evidence is so slender that it should not be taken too seriously. 'Maker unknown' means that to try to attach the name of a maker to these wares would be pure guesswork.

Whenever the words 'probably' or 'possibly' are used the reasons for doing so are given. It is regrettable that so few writers put forward their arguments for suggested attributions: it can only be helpful to collectors and occasionally leads someone to confirm or refute the arguments with further evidence. Reference to patterns illustrated in this book will be made by stating the number of the plate in brackets in the appropriate place. When reference is made to the following publications, which are quoted frequently, the author's name only will be used, followed by the number of the page or plate.

Coysh, A. W. *Blue and White Transfer Ware 1780-1840* (1970)

Godden, G. A. *Encyclopaedia of British Pottery and Porcelain Marks* (1964) (Abbreviated to GM followed by the number of the ceramic mark.)

Godden, G. A. *An Illustrated Encyclopaedia of British Pottery and Porcelain* (1966) (Abbreviated to GI followed by the number of the plate.)

Moore, W. Hudson. *The Old China Book* (1935 edition)

Little, W. L. *Staffordshire Blue* (1969)

Whiter, L. *Spode* (1970) (The author's name followed by a number refers to one of the Spode marks on pages 221-226)

Williams, S. B. *Antique Blue and White Spode* (1949 edition).

Other useful reference books include:

Adams, P. W. L. *A History of the Adams Family of North Staffordshire* (1914)

Bell, R. C. *Tyneside Pottery* (1971)

Barber, E. A. *Anglo-American Pottery* (Indianapolis 1899; Philadelphia 1901)

Camehl, A. W. *The Blue China Book* (New York, 1916; 1948)

Eaglestone, A. A. and Lockett, T. A. *The Rockingham Pottery* (Rotherham 1964; 1967)

Earle, A. M. *China Collecting in America* (1892)

Falkner, F. *The Wood Family of Burslem* (1912)

Fennley, C. *Something Blue: some American Views on Staffordshire* (Old Sturbridge, Mass. 1955; 1967)

Godden, G. A. *Mason's Patent Ironstone China* (1971)

Godden, G. A. *Minton Pottery and Porcelain of the First Period 1793-1850* (1968)

Grabham, O. *Yorkshire Potteries, Pots and Potters* (1916; 1971)

Haggar, R. G. *The Masons of Lane Delph* (1952)

Hayden, A. *Chats on English Earthenware* (1909; 1922); *Spode and his Successors* (1925)

Hillier, B. *The Turners of Lane End* (1965)

Hughes, G. B. *English and Scottish Earthenware* (1961); *Victorian Pottery and Porcelain* (1959; 1968)

Hurst, A. *A Catalogue of the Boynton Collection of Yorkshire Pottery* (York 1932)

Jewitt, A. *The Ceramic Art of Great Britain* (1878) (A reprint of the American edition published in New York in 1883 was issued by P. Minet of Chicheley in 1971, and a revised and expanded edition by G. A. Godden of those parts of the original edition dealing with the nineteenth century was issued by Barrie and Jenkins in 1972.)

Kidson, J. R. and F. *The Leeds Old Pottery* (1892; 1970)

Laidacker, S. *Anglo-American China* Parts 1 and 2 (Bristol Pennsylvania 1951)

Lancaster, H. B. *Liverpool and her Potters* (1936)

Larsen, E. B. *American Historical Views on Staffordshire China* (New York 1939)

Lockett, T. A. *Davenport Pottery and Porcelain 1794-1887* (1972)

Nance, E. M. *The Pottery and Porcelain of Swansea and Nantgarw* (1942)

Nicholls, R. *The Adams Family* (1928)

Peel, D. A. *Pride of Potters* (1957)

Pountney, W. J. *Old Bristol Potteries* (1920)

Rackham, B. *Leeds Pottery* (1938)

Rhead, G. W. *British Pottery Marks* (1910); *The Earthenware Collector* (1920)

Rhead, G. W. and F. A. *Staffordshire Pots and Potters* (1906)

Rice, D. G. *The Illustrated Guide to Rockingham Potteries* (1971)

Shaw, S. A. *A History of the Staffordshire Potteries* (1829; 1970)

Smith, A. *The Illustrated Guide to Liverpool Herculaneum Pottery* (1970)

Towner, D. C. *The Leeds Pottery* (1963)

Turner, W. *Transfer Printing on Enamels, Porcelain and Pottery* (1907); *William Adams, an old English Potter* (1923)

Wood, R. H. and V. A. *Historical China Cup Plates* (Baltimore, Md. no date)

MAKERS AND PATTERNS: 1800-1850

The Adams Family

Blue-printed ware made by members of the Adams family between 1800 and 1850 were of very high quality. At the beginning of this period three cousins, all called William Adams, were producing blue and white earthenwares in potteries at Cobridge, Tunstall and Stoke-on-Trent respectively. All three cousins had sons called William who joined their firms. Indeed, it has been said that to speak of William Adams in the Potteries at this time was like speaking of John Jones in a Welsh village. The fact that they all marked their wares ADAMS with or without an additional symbol, makes attribution to a particular factory difficult for the collector. Not that it matters greatly for no doubt the relatives helped one another in times of stress and worked to some extent as a large family business. Little (pp 42-5) gives a very useful genealogical tree showing the family relationships and a summary of the work of these potters.

William Adams of Cobridge was among the first potters in Staffordshire to produce blue-printed wares and his early designs were no doubt 'in the Chinese taste'. He had several potteries but he gave up potting in at least two of these before his final retirement. J. & R. Clews are said to have rented one of his Cobridge factories in 1818. Since Clews used a mark very similar to one of the Adams marks—i.e. the words WARRANTED STAFFORDSHIRE within concentric circles enclosing a crown (GM 20 and 919) and also used a fritillary border (18) previously used on Adams wares bearing this mark one wonders whether these were previously used by William Adams of Cobridge. We shall probably never know. However, it is just possible that the Rural Scenes (1 and 2) were produced at Cobridge.

William Adams of Greengates, Tunstall also started blue-printing at an early date. It is generally assumed that the impressed mark ADAMS was the mark of this member of the family but this occurs on wares with patterns that appear to have been produced well after his death in 1805. *The Native Pattern* (Coysh, plate 17) is a good example. His son took over the factory in 1809 and ran it until 1820 and during this period appears to have added his initial. Wares marked B. ADAMS (3) are therefore among the few wares produced by the Adams family which can be attributed with confidence.

William Adams of Stoke started to make blue-

1 (above left) Adams   Rural Scenes Series (A)
         Milking Time Pattern (A)
Slightly indented plate (c 1820-30), in very dark blue, with a scene of a woman milking a cow in front of a cottage. Another woman, carrying a child, holds out a bowl for milk. The scene is framed in a wide border of branches, leaves and flowers.
Impressed mark: ADAMS: WARRANTED STAFFORDSHIRE *between concentric circles which enclose a crown (variant of GM 20) Diam 25.7cm (10.1in). Double foot rim. Rippled blue glaze.*

2 (above right) Adams   Rural Scenes Series (A)
         Three Cows Pattern. (A)
Slightly indented plate (c 1820-30), in very dark blue, with a scenes of three cows in a field. A woman rides on horseback towards a wood with a man on foot beside her. The scene is framed in scrolls and vine leaves, part of a wide border of flowers and fruit on a stipple ground extending to the well of the plate.
Impressed mark: As in 1 above.
Diam 25.7cm (10.1in). Double foot rim. Rippled blue glaze.

3 (below left) Benjamin Adams of Greengates
         Tendril Pattern (A)
Indented plate (1809-20), in dark blue, with a stylised flower motif enclosed in a dark circular band. A similar band encircles the rim of the plate and between these bands is an overall pattern of stylised leaves and flowers linked by a mass of tendrils.
Impressed mark: B. ADAMS
Diam 24.6cm (9.7in). No foot rim. Pale blue rippled glaze.

4 (below right) William Adams & Son of Stoke
     Country House Series (A) Blenheim, Oxfordshire.
(Courtesy: Ian Henderson, Esq.)
Indented plate (c 1820-30), in dark blue, with a view of Blenheim Palace from the north-west set in parkland with deer and cattle. A stretch of water in the foreground carries three swans. The border is of flowers and scrolls against a fine-mesh net background.
Impressed mark: ADAMS *above an eagle with* WARRANTED STAFFORDSHIRE *completing a circle. (see GM 19)*
Printed mark: scrolls and leaves with the words
         BLENHEIM
         OXFORDSHIRE.
Diam 25.9cm (10.2in). Double foot rim. Very blue slightly rippled glaze.

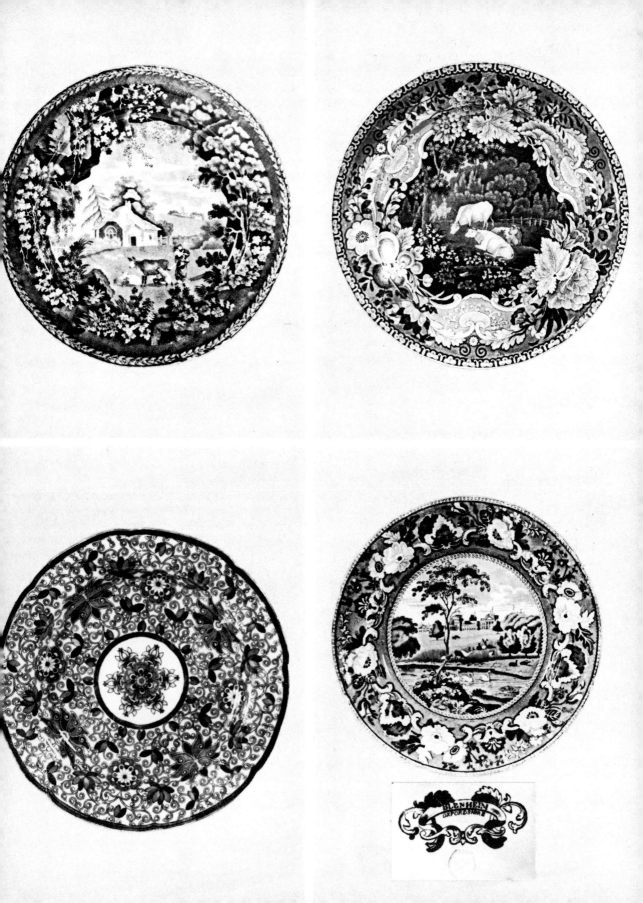

printed wares at Cliff Bank Works in 1804 and from 1819 began to take his sons into partnership when the firm became William Adams & Sons. The pottery had an important export trade, especially after 1821 when premises were opened in New York. Expansion continued for many years and in 1830 further offices were opened in Mexico and a Caribbean and South American trade developed. Although American views were produced it would seem that the earlier exports were of British views which could also be sold on the home market. These were of abbeys, castles and country houses. Some 27 different examples have been recorded in America (Moore p 273). All those examined have a double foot rim, an impressed mark with an eagle, and the name of the view, though borders vary.

The *Bird and Basket Chinoiserie Pattern* (5) and the *Lions Pattern* (6) carry the impressed mark ADAMS but it is difficult to believe that the latter was produced before 1809 when Adams of Greengates died. The lion design is based on two engravings in Jardine's *Natural History*.

Bathwell and Goodfellow

The partnership of Bathwell and Goodfellow operated two Potteries in Staffordshire: one at Burslem from 1818 to 1823 and the other at Tunstall from 1820 to 1822. Yet in this five year period they produced some good quality wares for both appear to have been experienced potters. The more important factory appears to have been the Upper House Works at Burslem which is sometimes recorded as that of 'Goodfellow and Bathwell.'

The examples show rural scenes similar to those used by Henshall & Co. (Little, plate 34) and an unknown potter (Coysh, plate 164). They are double-printed and carry the same border. Both have double foot rims and the same printed 'rock cartouche' with the words RURAL SCENERY (7). Although only one is impressed with the name of the maker there can be little doubt about the attribution of the other (8).

5 (above left) Probably William Adams of Greengates
Bird and Basket Chinoiserie Pattern (A)
(Courtesy: Robin Gurnett, Esq)
Indented plate (c 1810-20) in medium blue, with a central circular medallion with an exotic bird perched on the handle of a basket of flowers, the whole framed in a key-pattern-style surround. Outside are four scrolled panels, each with three Chinese figures, the opposite panels matching. They are linked by scrolls and irregular mosaic motifs with a mosaic groundwork. There is a dark blue band around the edge of the rim with a chain-link motif.
Impressed mark: ADAMS
Diam 25.4cm (10in). No foot rim. Base slightly concave. Colourless rippled glaze.

6 (above right) Probably William Adams & Sons
The Lions Pattern (A)
Slightly indented plate (c 1830), in medium to dark blue, with a woodland scene with a lion, lioness and two cubs. The border is of flowers and leaves against a stipple ground covered with very small florets. A stringing of formalised leaves separates the pattern from the border.
Impressed mark: ADAMS.
Diam 21.3cm (8.8in). Single foot rim. Deep blue rippled glaze on white body.

7 (below left) Bathwell & Goodfellow
'Rural Scenery Series': The Firewood Pattern (A)
(Courtesy: Robin Gurnett, Esq)
Indented dished plate (1818-23) with a double-printed scene in light and dark blue of a villager carrying poles and approaching a woman holding a faggot in her hands. A child is seated. In the distance are some thatched buildings. A border of flowers and leaf-scrolls on a stipple ground extends to the well of the plate. There is dentil stringing around the rim.
Impressed mark: BATHWELL & GOODFELLOW arranged to form an oval.
Printed mark: RURAL SCENERY in a cartouche of trees and rocks.
Diam 24.4cm (9.6in). Double foot rim. Rippled blue glaze.

8 (below right) Attributed to Bathwell & Goodfellow
'Rural Scenery Series': The Reaper Pattern (A)
(Courtesy: Robin Gurnett, Esq)
Indented plate (1818-23) with a double-printed scene in light and dark blue of a reaper with a reaping hook leaving a woman and child. In the distance are thatched buildings. Border as in 7.
Printed mark: RURAL SCENERY (as in 7)
Diam 24.9 (9.8in). Double foot rim. Rippled blue glaze.

RURAL
SCENERY

Bo'ness Pottery of West Lothian, Scotland

Bo'ness Pottery was established in the late eighteenth century in the parish of Borrowstouness and Carriden which lies on the southern shores of the Firth of Forth in West Lothian, some 24 miles from Edinburgh. The pottery was run by at least four different owners before it was purchased in 1836 by J. Jamieson & Co. (Note the spelling. Some writers refer to the firm incorrectly as Jameson & Co.) At this time a decision was made to manufacture blue-printed wares and experienced workers in this field were brought from Staffordshire. The best known pattern was *Bosphorus* (9) which is said to have sold well, but the quality of the wares is inferior to early Staffordshire wares. Jamieson died in 1854 and the pottery was then taken over by John Marshall.

Brameld & Co of Swinton Old Pottery, Yorkshire

Between 1787 and 1806 the Swinton Old Pottery was linked with Leeds Old Pottery, first as Greens, Bingley & Co, and after 1800 as Greens, Hartley & Co. In 1806 the association with Leeds was severed and John Brameld took over in partnership with his son, William, as Brameld & Co. In 1813 John Brameld died and his son succeeded him. In 1820 the firm started to manufacture porcelain and in 1826 became the Rockingham China Works.

Most of the blue-printd wares bear the impressed mark BRAMELD and some of the patterns were undoubtedly produced in the 1806 to 1826 period before the pottery became a 'China Works'. However, the factory continued to produce earthenwares until 1842. There is some doubt about the marks used on earthenwares after 1826. Some were certainly marked Rockingham but in the view of the author the BRAMELD mark was continued, at least on dinner services, well into the 1830s.

The *Woodman Pattern* (10), *Sweet Pea Pattern* (11) and the *Castle of Rochefort Pattern* (Coysh, plate 78) are examples of early productions. These designs cover most of the surface of the wares and are typical of the 1806-26 period.

It is interesting to note the shapes used for the dinner services printed with these patterns. The *Castle of Rochefort Pattern* appears on round plates and oval dishes, the *Woodman Pattern* and the *Sweet Pea Pattern* were printed on eight-sided plates and dishes (see D. G. Rice. *The Illustrated*

9 (above) Bo'ness Pottery, West Lothian
'Bosphorus' Pattern
Eight-sided indented dish (c 1840), in medium blue, with a Turkish-style scene with minarets beside water. Two figures are central in the foreground, one standing and smoking a long-stemmed pipe. The border which extends to the well of the plate is of flowers and leaves on a blue ground.
Impressed mark: PORCELAINE OPAQUE
J. JAMIESON & CO.
BO'NESS
within an oval. There is also an impressed 12 and a star.
Printed mark: BOSPHORUS on a ribbon beneath which is a second ribbon with the name of the maker in smaller capitals—J. JAMIESON & CO. Above the ribbon is an anchor.
Length 35.2cm (13.8in). Width 30cm (11.8 in). No foot rim. Smooth pale blue glaze.

10 (below left) Brameld & Co   'Woodman Pattern'
(Courtesy: Mr and Mrs J. G. Evans)
Dished octagonal plate (c 1806-26), in dark blue, with a scene of a woodman returning to his cottage and being greeted by his child. The mother is seated outside the cottage with her spinning wheel. The narrow printed border gives the impression of scrolled gadrooning.
Impressed mark: BRAMELD in small capitals within a cartouche.
Diam 25.4cm (10in). Shallow rounded foot rim Colourless rippled glaze.

11 (below right) Brameld & Co
'Sweet Pea Pattern'
(Courtesy: Robin Gurnett, Esq)
Octagonal plate (c 1806-26), in medium and dark blue, with an overall pattern of sweet pea flowers, leaves and tendrils on a stipple ground, the whole enclosed in a blue band with dentil decoration.
Impressed mark: BRAMELD within a cartouche.
Diam 24.4cm (9.6in). Single foot rim. Smooth blue glaze with a few small bubbles near rim.

Guide to Rockingham Pottery and Porcelain. 1971. Plates 16-18.)

Floral patterns which leave large areas of the ware unprinted were probably introduced in the 1820s. Two examples are given here—the *Twisted Tree Pattern* (12) and the *Parroquet Pattern* (13). The twisted tree derives from a Chinese design though such patterns are often associated with the name Indian. The Spode *India Pattern* (Coysh, plate 113), for example, is in the same style as a pattern known as 'Indian Tree' which is still used by several firms today.

The *Twisted Tree Pattern* (12) seems to have been a dual-purpose production. It is often found as a blue-printed pattern but in some cases the outlines have been subsequently filled in to produce a coloured design, presumably at the factory. It is found on stone china.

The *Parroquet Pattern* (13) differs from the Twisted Tree pattern in that the flowers instead of being left largely in outline with little shading are given 'depth' by skilful use of stipple engraving. This example of stone china is interesting. The Old Swinton Pottery must have produced a number of heavier bodies for other names of the same type occur from time to time on their wares—GRANITE CHINA, STONE CHINA, FINE STONE and INDIA STONE CHINA have all been recorded.

The most interesting designs produced by Brameld & Co, are those based on the illustrations by Thomas Stothard (1755-1834) prepared for an edition of Cervantes' *Don Quixote* published by Harrison & Co, of London in 1782. Stothard, the son of a London innkeeper, served as an apprentice in the workshop of a pattern-drawer. He became a painter and book illustrator, was elected to the Royal Academy in 1794 and became the Academy Librarian in 1812. His designs were highly imaginative. A single dinner service depicting the amusing adventures of Don Quixote and Sancho Panza included many scenes. These designs were probably introduced early in the 1830s for they are often printed in green. In this respect the series may be compared with Spode's *Aesop's Fables* (p 80). It should be noted that J. & R. Clews is said to have produced a Don Quixote series prior to 1834 for the American market with 21 different designs. (Moore p 263).

The unmarked dish (14) shows Don Quixote falling from his horse when tilting at windmills. The windmills extend to the horizon as though reflected in double mirrors. D. G. Rice illustrates many pieces from a green-printed dinner service

12 (above) Brameld & Co   *'Twisted Tree Pattern'*
(Courtesy: Mr and Mrs J. G. Evans)
Slightly indented dished plate (c 1820-30), in medium blue, with a so-called 'twisted tree' with leaves and flowers. A bird and an insect also form part of the design which covers the whole plate.
Impressed mark: BRAMELD *in small capitals, within a cartouche.*
Diam 25.4cm (10in). Very shallow rounded foot rim. Colourless rippled glaze.

13 (below) Brameld & Co   *'Parroquet Pattern'*
(Courtesy: Mr and Mrs J. G. Evans)
Twelve-sided dish with gadrooned edge (c 1820-30), each side slightly curved, printed in dark blue with a central design with foliage and flowers and two 'parroquets'. The border is discontinuous and consists of four groups of flowers and foliage.
Impressed mark: BRAMELD +1
Printed mark: A bird beneath which are the words 'Parroquet Fine Stone': Below this is a letter B.
Length 54.6cm (21.5in). Width 41.3cm (16.25in). No foot rim. Colourless rippled glaze.

(*ibid.* plates 27a to 27g) in which at least a dozen different scenes may be seen and anyone familiar with Don Quixote could no doubt identify the various episodes. It would be useful to compile a list of known Don Quixote patterns. Although most of the pieces bear the mark BRAMELD, many are unmarked. However, they all bear the characteristic discontinuous border of floral sprays within C-scrolls and are easily recognised.

Thomas and John Carey

Wares marked CAREYS vary enormously in type and quality. Two different bodies were used—a fine pearlware with well printed patterns such as *The Lady of the Lake* (Coysh, plate 19), and a very heavy stoneware sometimes called 'Saxon Stone' which was used for dinner services, printed sometimes in brown, sometimes in blue. It was used for Carey's *Cathedral Series* of which G. A. Godden illustrates a good example in *The Illustrated Guide to Mason's Patent Ironstone China*. 1971. Plate 106. The example with the chinoiserie pattern (15) is thickly potted and weighs over 3½ lbs. These Saxon Stone wares were probably made towards the end of the Careys partnership between about 1830 and 1842.

Castleford Pottery

This pottery was established in about 1790 by David Dunderdale who had been an apprentice at Leeds Old Pottery. From about 1793 it continued as David Dunderdale & Co until about 1820. The Castleford Pottery is best known for its white felspar stoneware teapots but it also produced blue-printed wares with chinoiserie decoration. *The Buffalo and Ruins Pattern* (16) has much in common with the Davenport *Chinoiserie Ruins Pattern* (Coysh, plate 26) including the trees, fence and figure with a parasol. The buffalo resembles that in the early *Buffalo Pattern* (Coysh, plate 2).

14 (*above*) Attributed to Brameld & Co
'Don Quixote Series'
Tilting at Windmills (A)
(*Courtesy: Mr and Mrs J. G. Evans*)
Indented dish (c 1830-35) with prominently moulded C-scroll edge, printed in medium blue with a view of Don Quixote tilting at windmills. The border is divided into four distinct panels each with a spray of flowers within a plain C-scroll of colour.
Impressed mark: 18
Length 47.3cm (19in). Width 38.1cm (15in). No foot rim. Smooth colourless glaze.

15 (*below left*) Thomas and John Carey
Bridge and Pagoda Pattern (A)
(*Courtesy: Robin Gurnett, Esq*)
Twelve-sided gadrooned stoneware tureen stand (c 1830-42) in medium blue, with a view in which a three-storey pagoda by a river bank is approached by steps from the water or by a bridge crossing the water. Two men stand on the first floor verandah of the pagoda and three men stand on the opposite bank of the river. A man in a rowing boat approaches the steps. Two palm trees dominate the scene. The border repeats the main features of the central view and is separated from the gadrooned edge of the stand by a line-engraved band with clover leaf motifs.
Impressed mark: CAREYS *beneath an anchor.*
Diam 33.8cm (13.3in). Prominent foot rim. Thick milky-white glaze on brownish stoneware body.

16 (*below right*) Castleford Pottery
Buffalo and Ruins Pattern (A)
Indented plate (c 1800-20), in medium blue, with a chinoiserie pattern with tropical trees and a gothic ruin. The scene includes two fences, a two-arch bridge with a figure carrying a parasol, and a man mounted on a buffalo pointing towards a man seated on the ground. The border repeats the tropical trees and leaves motif.
Impressed mark: D.D. & CO.
CASTLEFORD
POTTERY
Diam 23.5cm (9.2in). No foot rim. Colourless rippled glaze.

Chetham & Robinson of Longton

The kidney-shaped dish (17) is of particularly good quality—well potted and well glazed. The engraving is crisp with a good combination of stipple and line. The shape follows that used from time to time for Caughley and Derby porcelains in the last quarter of the eightenth century. The mark shows the letters C. & R. within a Staffordshire knot. These initials have been used by two different firms—Chesworth & Robinson of Lane End, Staffordshire from 1825 to 1840 and Chetham and Robinson of Commercial Street, Longton from 1822 to 1837. The attribution of wares with this pattern and mark is therefore in doubt. The tentative choice of Chetham & Robinson has been made since wares of such good quality must have been made by experienced potters and a Chetham partnership had existed since 1796. We know less about Chesworth and Robinson but it would appear that the firm started under that name in 1825, though G. A. Godden states that they were 'formerly Chesworth & Wood'. In any case, this is one of the earliest known of ceramic marks with the Staffordshire knot which was not common until the 1840s.

17 (above) Probably Chetham and Robinson
Parkland Scenery Pattern (A)
(Courtesy: Robin Gurnett, Esq)
Kidney-shaped dish (c1822-37), in medium and dark blue, with a parkland scene with a country mansion seen across a stretch of water on which there is a sailing boat with three figures. In the foreground a man stands talking to a seated woman with a boy at her side. The picture is framed in a cusped white band. The border of flowers is on a fine-mesh net ground.
Printed mark: WARRANTED with the letters C & R within a Staffordshire knot which throws a shadow.
Length 27.6cm (10.9in). Prominent foot rim. Smooth blue glaze.
17a (above right) Mark on base of No. 17 and border of a dinner plate with the Parkland Scenery Pattern (A)

James & Ralph Clews of Cobridge

This firm which operated from 1817 to 1834 had a large output (Coysh, pp 22-4) among which were dinner services with views of abbeys, castles and cathedrals. These included a view of Fonthill Abbey in Wiltshire (18) as seen from the south-west. The abbey was built by William Thomas Beckford (1760-1844). In 1793 he planned the building with the architect, James Wyatt, which was to be like a medieval monastery with a tower 278 feet high. It took many years to build but was completed in 1813. Ten years later, Beckford was in financial trouble and sold the abbey. In 1825 the tower collapsed and the building lay in ruins. (See Brockman, H. A. N. The Caliph of Fonthill. 1956.) Assuming that the dish was made when the tower was still standing it can be dated to between 1817 and 1825.

Moore lists other views in this Clews series which were among the wares exported to America.
Dulwich Castle; Lumley Castle, Durham; Rothesay Castle, Buteshire; St. Mary's Abbey, York; Stratford-on-Avon, Warwickshire; Warkworth Castle, Northumberland; and Wells Cathedral, Somerset.

18 (below) J. & R. Clews
'Fonthill Abbey, Wiltshire'.
Eight-sided indented dish (c 1817-25) in medium blue, with a view of William Beckford's Fonthill Abbey in Wiltshire seen from the south-west. The foreground shows part of the estate landscaped with trees and avenues. The border of flowers (including fritillaries) on a stipple ground extends to the well of the dish and is separated from the central view by stringing.
Impressed mark: STAFFORDSHIRE. CLEWS WARRANTED between concentric circles which enclose a crown (GM 919)
Printed mark: FONTHILL ABBEY, WILT-SHIRE within an oval band with flowers.
Length 43.2cm (17in). Width 33.1cm (12.9in). No foot rim. Pale blue rippled glaze.

Copeland and Garrett of Stoke

When Josiah Spode III died in 1829 the Spode works at Stoke-on-Trent were continued by the trustees until 1833 when William Taylor Copeland took over the pottery. He formed a partnerhip with Thomas Garrett and the firm traded under the names of Copeland & Garrett (late Spode) until 1847. During this period a number of new patterns were launched and many of the earlier Spode designs were continued. Blue-printing, however, declined in importance and many of the dinner services were printed in green instead. The Aesop's Fables series (see pp 80-1), for example, appeared in green.

One of the most interesting new series with an attractive border of scrolled leaves (20) was of named *Italian Views—Mount Etna, The Tiber, Venice*, etc. These views, however, are not true topographical scenes. They were not taken from illustrations in books of travel as were the earlier Spode Italian patterns (Coysh, pp 76-9) but were greatly influenced by the imagination of the artists.

Another striking feature of the designs of the 1830s was the inclusion of a massive urn in the foreground. This is found, for example, in the Copeland & Garrett *Seasons* series (19) and in the Pountney & Allies *Fancy Vase Pattern* (70)

Technical improvements continued during the Copeland and Garrett period and the marks, which usually have the name of the firm printed in a circle, sometimes include the name of the body e.g. 'New Fayence' (continued from the Spode period), 'New Blanche' or 'New Japan Stone'.

Walter Daniel of Burslem

Walter Daniel operated the Newport Pottery at Burslem from about 1786 and sold the works to John Davenport about 1810. The rare marked plate (21) which must have been made between these dates, has a border very like the Leeds Old Pottery and Cambrian Pottery two-man scroll patterns (Coysh, plates 10 and 12). The central scene, however, has the true willow tree and also two birds. The pagodas are unusual in style and there is a woman with parasol in the foreground—hence the adopted name. The plate has a very fine glaze and a good colour, both reminiscent of early wares of the Leeds Old Pottery.

19 (above) Copeland & Garrett
'The Seasons' Series 'Spring on Richmond Hill'
(Courtesy: Mr and Mrs Martin Pulver)
Eight-sided indented dish (1833-47), in medium blue, with a scene on Richmond Hill. The River Thames is seen in the distance, figures dance round the maypole on the hill. The foreground has a flight of steps and large vase of spring flowers bearing the word 'SPRING'. The border of C-scrolls on a dark ground has four elongated panels with a geometrical motif and four scrolled medallions, each symbolic of one of the four seasons.
Impressed mark: COPELAND & GARRETT in a circle enclosing the words LATE SPODE.
Printed mark: COPELAND
                   AND
                   GARRETT
         STOKE UPON TRENT
                   &
               LONDON
This is printed on a shield within draped curtains (cf GM 1095). Below the shield are the words RICHMOND HILL and CHINA GLAZE. Length 53.3cm (21in). Width 39.4cm (15.5in). No foot rim. Smooth pale blue glaze.
20 (below left) Copeland & Garrett
         Italian Scenes (A) 'Mount Etna' pattern
(Courtesy: Robin Gurnett, Esq)
Tureen stand (1833-47), in a medium blue, with a distant view of Mount Etna seen across a landscape with bridge, trees, horned sheep and peasants. The view is framed in a border of scrolled acanthus-type leaves in two bands on a clover-leaf ground.
Impressed mark: COPELAND & GARRETT in a circle enclosing the words LATE SPODE.
Printed mark: as above with MOUNT ETNA on a scroll beneath (cf GM1092)
Diam 18.5cm (7.3in). Rounded foot rim. Smooth pale blue glaze.
21 (below right) Walter Daniel of Burslem
         The Parasol Willow Pattern (A)
(Courtesy: Mr and Mrs Martin Pulver)
Indented plate (c 1800), in dark blue, with bridgeless willow pattern which includes a large chinese building with a pier-like structure built out across the water. A large boat with a superstructure flies a pennant. A woman carrying an open parasol walks in front of the pagoda with a child. The picture is framed in a band of small circles broken in six places by star-shaped flower heads. The border is of geometrical motifs, flowers and Chinese writing scrolls.
Impressed mark: W. DANIEL
Diam 25.4cm (10in). No foot rim. Pale bluish-green rippled glaze.

Davenport of Longport

The Davenport family potted in Staffordshire from 1794 until 1887. During this period the firm traded under the following names:

c 1785-1830   John Davenport (retired 1830)

1830-1835   Henry and William Davenport (the sons)

1835-1869   William Davenport & Co

The marks include the single name DAVENPORT so it is not always easy to date pieces accurately. The common mark is an impressed anchor which, after about 1835, carried date numerals. Some marks, however, are printed and only carry the name Davenport. Most of the finer blue-printed wares belong to the 1794-1830 period and many of them have already been illustrated (Coysh, plates 26-35).

The plate (22) is an example from another group of country scenes. This shows gothic ruins in a rural setting. Little illustrates another example (plate 23) with the same border.

The *Legend of Montrose* plate (23) carries the date 1840, though other examples have been noted in the *Scott's Illustrations Series* with the earlier date of 1836. In the 1830s it was fashionable to bind up the illustrations engraved for books of famous authors in separate volumes. A book entitled *Illustrations of the Waverley Novels*, for example, was published in 1833 and no doubt inspired this Davenport series of patterns. Again, a keen collector might well compile a list of Davenport patterns in the *Scott's Illustrations Series*.

The *Florentine Fountain Pattern* (24) probably dates from the 1830s. It has already been pointed out that large urns often feature in patterns of this period. The same is true of large fountains which were equally popular when designs were specially drawn for blue-printed wares. In the mid-1830s the Davenport firm began to depart from the 'blue' tradition. Services were already being produced in two colours in 1835 and services in green were available by 1836. Nevertheless, for many wares intended mainly for practical purposes blue continued as the main colour. These included mugs, feeding cups, pap boats, spittoons, bordaloues and toilet wares. The pap boat (25) is a good example. No great effort was made to produce new engravings. Many of them carry the *Muleteer Pattern* (Coysh, plate 35). The border of this pap boat, for example, carries a pattern which was used with the Muleteer design. 'Pap', incidentally, which was used for feeding infants, was simply bread soaked

22 (above left) John Davenport
Gothic Ruins Pattern (A)
(Courtesy: Robin Gurnett, Esq)
Indented plate (c 1810-20), in medium blue, with a rustic scene dominated by a gothic ruin. A man and a woman in the foreground stand beside a second man seated on a mound or rock. A sailing ship on a distant stretch of water flies a long pennant. The border is of flowers and leaves against a stipple ground.
Impressed mark: Davenport (in lower case letters) above an anchor (GM1181)
Diam 24.6cm (9.7in). No foot rim. Clean colourless glaze.

23 (above right) William Davenport & Co
'Scotts Illustrations' Series
'Legend of Montrose'
(Courtesy: Mr and Mrs Martin Pulver)
Slightly indented plate (1840), in medium blue, with a scene in which two Scots in kilts appear to be fighting over a diminutive female figure. The border of C-scrolls, roses and passion flowers descends to the well of the plate.
Impressed mark: DAVENPORT curving above an anchor with the year figures 4 and 0 on either side and the figure 6 above.
Printed mark: 'Scotts Illustrations' and 'Legend of Montrose' within a cartouche of C-scrolls. Below is the name DAVENPORT.
Diam 22.9cm (9in). Double foot rim. Smooth colourless glaze.

24 (below) Probably Henry & William Davenport
'Florentine Fountain' Pattern
Indented dish (c 1830-35), double printed in light and dark blue, with an imaginary scene which includes a prominent fountain surmounted by a statue of a crowned kneeling figure holding a trident. On a rococo bridge stands a woman with a pitcher on her head. The border is moulded with a slight ridge on the rim opposite each indentation. The border pattern is of butterflies and flowers.
Impressed mark: DAVENPORT above an anchor, the whole surmounted by a figure 3.
Printed mark: 'Florentine Fountain' within a cartouche of flowers with a fountain. Also separately printed DAVENPORT.
Length 37.5cm (14.7in). Width 30cm (11.8in). No foot rim. Gritty colourless glaze.

in milk and water, or in water alone. This was fed to the infant in the pap boat with the lip placed to the mouth. A number of other firms produced blue-printed pap boats of this type including Minton and Wedgwood.

Davenport wares have been described in T. A. Lockett's *Davenport Pottery and Porcelain 1794-1887.* (David & Charles, Newton Abbot, 1972.)

Deakin & Bailey of Lane End

Little is known about this Staffordshire pottery which is said to have been in production from c 1828 to c 1830 and to have used printed marks incorporating the latters D. & B. (see GM4420). The plate with the *Villa Scenery Pattern* (26) is of very good quality—well potted and moulded and accurately double-printed. The printing fits very neatly against the moulding on the rim. Double printing was already being used by a number of potters after about 1825.

The letters 'D. & B' are said to have been used by the Stepney pottery of Dalton & Burn at Ouseburn on Tyneside but this pottery did not appear in local directories as Dalton & Burn until 1844. It was previously known as Dalton, Burn & Co (see Bell, R. C. *Tyneside Pottery.* 1971. p 54).

Thomas Dimmock & Co

The letter 'D' appearing in printed marks is normally attributed to Thomas Dimmock & Co which had several works in the Potteries—a large works at Hanley and two at Shelton, in Albion Street and Tontine Street respectively.
They operated from c 1828 to c 1850 though the Albion Street works may have continued until 1859. Several Dimmock marks are listed by Godden (GM 1297-1301) who incidentally points out that there were other potters by the name of Dimmock working in the area at the same time.

The example illustrated (27) is not of particularly good quality. The dish is thickly potted and the printing is far from crisp. However, the subject is of some interest, particularly to those who collect 'named views'. The Menai Suspension Bridge was opened in 1825. The design was by Thomas Telford (1757-1834). (See Smiles, S. *Lives of the Engineers.* 1861. Vol II.)

25 (above left) William Davenport & Co
'Muleteer Border' Pattern
(Courtesy: The Wellcome Trustees)
Pap-boat (c 1835-50), in medium blue, with a pattern of scrolls and flowers based on that used with the Muleteer pattern but including two small birds.
Printed mark: DAVENPORT and the number 2.
Length 11.1cm (4.4in). Width 6cm (2.35in). Height 4.6cm (1.8in)

26 (above right) probably Deakin & Bailey
'Villa Scenery' Pattern
Moulded plate (c 1828-30), printed in medium and dark blue, with an Italian-style scene with a classical building, lake and mountains. The foreground is of flowers with a prominent thrush-like bird. The moulded rim bears twelve five-petalled flowers against which scrolls and cellular motifs are printed in dark blue. From these scrolls, floral sprays, some of which include passion flowers, descend towards the well of the plate.
Printed mark: A scroll bearing the words 'Villa Scenery', and the letters D. & B. held in the beak of a bird perched on a stone.
Diam 25.9cm (10.2in). Rounded foot rim. Smooth pale blue glaze.

27 (below) Probably Thomas Dimmock & Co
'Select Sketches' Series
'Menai Bridge'
(Courtesy: Ian Henderson, Esq)
Indented vegetable dish base (c 1830-40), in medium blue, with a view inside (left) of the Menai Bridge across the Menai Strait. There are ships on the river and a man, woman, and child with dog in the foreground. The border is of scrolls and geometrical motifs against a stipple ground and swags of flowers descent towards the well of the dish. The border is repeated around the sides of the dish. The handles are printed in a lighter blue stipple. The lid is divided by a scrolled border into four panels, two with sprays of flowers and two with a river scene with bridge, steps and church.
Diam of dish 26.8cm (10.5in). Overall height with lid 17.8cm (7in). Foot rim 2.5cm (1in). Smooth pale blue glaze.

Don Pottery

The Don Pottery at Swinton in Yorkshire was an important firm in the first quarter of the nineteenth century and as Hurst points out in his *Catalogue of the Boynton Collection* (pp 16-17) 'probably turned out more ware than any other in the county with the exception of Leeds Old Pottery and employed between 200 and 300 workmen'. The best known printed patterns are those in the *Named Italian Views Series* (Coysh, pp 32-5). The patterns illustrated on the opposite page (28, 29 and 30) do not appear to have been described previously in detail though Alwyn and Angela Cox in an article in the *Collectors Guide* for November 1970 (p 91) refer to 'Italian-style scenes . . . enclosed by an arcaded border'. Examples to be seen in Doncaster Museum, printed not only in blue but also in black, are labelled under the general title 'Landscape'. Although the *Castello St Angelo Pattern* (28) is of an actual scene in Rome (see also Spode's *Tiber Pattern*, Coysh, plate 106), the others (29 and 30) appear to be imaginary scenes of the type which were popular on wares of the 1830-1850 period.

This series is certainly later than the *Named Italian Views*. The marks examined on wares with these two series differ. In the marks on *Named Italian Views* the lion often carries a rectangular flag; in the *Landscape* series the lion carries a swallow-tailed pennant. The *Landscape* series was almost certainly introduced in the John William Green & Co period which lasted from 1822 until 1833.

There is no evidence as yet to suggest that other potters used the *Landscape* patterns but since the *Named Italian Views* were described (Coysh, pp 32-5) at least some of these patterns have been noted on wares impressed with the name of TWIGG (see pp 88-9), though the quality of the prints is greatly inferior. Thirteen Don Pottery patterns in the *Named Italian Views* series have now been recorded. These include the Tomb of Aggrigentun (Little, plate 101), View of Alicata (Doncaster Museum); Ruins of the Castle Ca. . . .(?) (Doncaster Museum); Obelisk at Catania; Ancient Cistern at Catania (*Collectors Guide* Nov. 1970 p 90); View of Cerigliano (footbath in Doncaster Museum with this view inside and the view of the Residence of Solimenes outside); Monastery at Fra Castagne; Cascade at Isola; View of Palma (Coysh, plate 37); Temple of Serapis at Pouzzueli (?); Residence of Solimenes near Vesuvius (Coysh, plate 36); View

*28 (above left) Don Pottery   The 'Landscape' Series
Castello St. Angelo Pattern (A)*
Indented plate (c 1820-33), in medium blue, with a scene of the River Tiber at Rome with the Castle of St Angelo as a central feature. There are two figures and a dog in the foreground, and a boat with two figures sails on the river. The border is of floral medallions linked together to give an arcaded appearance.
Impressed mark: DON POTTERY, *also* L
Printed mark of a lion erased carrying a swallow-tailed pennant with the word 'DON'. The word 'POTTERY' appears beneath the lion. (a variant of GM1314).
Diam 25.4cm (10in). Double foot rim. Smooth blue glaze.

*29 (above right) Attributed to Don Pottery
The 'Landscape' Series
Reading Woman Pattern (A)*
Sauce boat (c 1820-33), in medium blue, with an Italian-style scene in which a woman stands beside a lake with a book in her left hand from which she appears to be reading to a boy. The background has several buildings. Elongated floral medallions decorate the ends of the sauce boat.
Unmarked.
Length 16.5cm (6.5in). Height to top of handle 8.9cm (3.5in). Smooth colourless glaze.

*30 (below) Don Pottery   The 'Landscape' Series.
Italian Fountain Pattern (A)*
Six-sided indented dish (c 1820-33), in medium blue, with an Italian-style scene with a building, lake and fountain. Two figures stand in the foreground. The border is of floral medallions linked together to give an arcaded appearance.
Printed mark: Crest mark of a lion erased carrying a swallow-tailed pennant with the word 'DON'. The word 'POTTERY' appears beneath the lion (A variant of GM1314).
Impressed mark: 16 and an asterisk.
Length 43.2cm (17in). Width 35.0cm (13.8in). Smooth colourless glaze.

near Taormina; Terrace of the Naval Amphitheatre at ... ?

The Don Pottery *Broseley Pattern* (31) appears to be identical to that used by the Coalport Factory on porcelain c 1810-15 (See G. A. Godden, *Collectors Guide*, February, 1968 Fig VII p 46) except that the design is reversed. This is also true of the identical Spode *Broseley* pattern (see Whiter plate 18) which was produced c 1818, also on porcelain. This reversal of pattern is not uncommon when a pattern has been copied and would seem to indicate that the copy was made from a transfer paper.

Elkin & Co of Lane End

The name 'Elkin' occurs in the title of a number of Staffordshire firms operating between 1820 and 1850. Of these, Elkin & Co of Lane End appears to be the earliest. The coffee can (32) which has a rare mark, is of good quality and dates from about 1822-30. It has been suggested (GM1468a) that there was a Knight in the partnership at this period and that Elkin & Co was Elkin, Knight and Elkin. One fact seems to be well established. Some time in the early 1820s a new works was built at Fenton which came to be known as Foley Potteries and was operated first by Elkin, Knight & Co (1822-6) and then by Elkin, Knight and Bridgwood (1827-40). Some blue-printed wares made by the latter have already been illustrated (Coysh, plates 39-41).

Thomas Fell & Co of Newcastle

A tea bowl and saucer by Thomas Fell & Co of Newcastle was illustrated in Coysh, plate 42. The tea cup and saucer (33) have been printed in the same dark blue. The cup corresponds closely to Spode's London shape dated c 1813 (Whiter, p 125). Although an anchor mark has been used by a number of other potteries there can be little doubt about the attribution since R. C. Bell in his book on *Tyneside Pottery* (1971) illustrates a similar anchor with the Fell initial 'F' on a saucer showing two people having tea in a garden (Mark M33, page 140). This pattern was also used but in reverse and with a different border by William Smith & Co of Stafford Pottery, Stockton-on-Tees (see GI 525) This type of scene was commonly used on tea-wares made in the Tyne-Tees potteries.

31 (*above left*) Don Pottery   Broseley Pattern (A)
Plate (c 1820-33) with scalloped edge, in light blue, with a willow pattern showing two men on a single-arch bridge facing a large pagoda. Five 'apple' trees appear on this pattern. The border is of geometrical motifs and insects.
Impressed mark: M.
Printed mark: Crest mark of a lion erased carrying a swallow-tailed pennant and the words DON POTTERY (variant of GM1314).
Diam 21cm (8.3in). No foot rim. Pale blue rippled glaze.

32 (*above right*) Elkin & Co   Pastoral Pattern (A)
(*Courtesy: Robin Gurnett, Esq*)
Coffee cup (c 1822-30) in medium blue, with a pastoral scene in which a shepherd sits resting with his dog beneath a tree in a fenced field with sheep and cattle. A border of roses and leaves on a dark blue ground extends 2.5cm (1in) from the rim inside the cup, and a fragment of this border decorates the handle.
Printed mark: ELKIN & CO. within a wreath of leaves.
Height to rim 4.8cm (1.9in). Diam 5.1cm (2in). Flattened foot rim. Smooth blue glaze.

33 (*below*) Attributed to Thomas Fell & Co
                Garden Pattern (A)
(*Courtesy: Robin Gurnett, Esq*)
Saucer (1817-30) in dark blue, with a garden scene in which a lady and gentleman are seated at a table beneath a tree. On the table is a jug. The man smokes a pipe while the lady holds a book. A dog lies at their feet. The border of wild roses and scrolls carries small oval medallions.
Impressed mark: B above an anchor. To the left of the anchor is a figure 1 and to the right a figure 4.
Diam 13.4cm (5.25in). Rounded foot rim. Pale blue slightly 'gritty' glaze.
The cup has medallions which carry the garden scene as on the saucer. The border inside the cup is also as on the saucer. Inside the base of the cup is a small scene with buildings, including a round tower.

Ferrybridge or Knottingley Pottery, Yorkshire

The Knottingley Pottery was established in 1792 on a site about two miles north-east of Pontefract. It operated as William Tomlinson & Co. In 1796 Ralph Wedgwood of Burslem (a nephew of Josiah Wedgwood) became a partner and the firm became Tomlinson, Foster, Wedgwood & Co, but marked its wares WEDGWOOD & CO, no doubt to take advantage of the name which was already famous in the pottery industry. Ralph Wedgwood set high standards and some fine wares were produced. The plate (34) is a good example: well potted, crisply printed and with a particularly fine glaze. Unfortunately, his experiments were costly and as a result the partnership broke up c 1801. The firm again became Tomlinson & Co. Three years later, in 1804, the name of the pottery was changed to Ferrybridge.

For some years the Ferrybridge Pottery continued to be operated by the Tomlinson family. William Tomlinson was succeeded by his son Edward who retired in 1826. It then became Reed, Taylor & Kelsall; in 1838 Reed, Taylor & Co, and in 1841 the Ferrybridge Pottery Co. The plate (35) with its classical scene was almost certainly made after 1804 when the firm had become Tomlinson & Co. From 1804 until 1826 the mark FERRYBRIDGE was used.

Thomas Godwin of Burslem Wharf

Thomas Godwin of Burslem, Staffordshire, succeeded Thomas & Benjamin Godwin in 1834 and within a few years had established a considerable export trade to America. The dish (36) with the view of *Boston and Bunkers Hill* is a typical example of his blue-printed export wares. Bunkers Hill was where the battle was fought in 1775 between colonists and the British Forces under General Gage during the American War of Independence. These dinner services all carried the border of morning glory and nasturtiums and were produced also in brown, green and red. According to Moore (p 275) views on Godwin's series also included Brooklyn Ferry; the City of Baltimore (GI277) Columbia Bridge, Pennsylvania; Schuylkill Water Works; The Capitol, Washington; The Narrows, Fort Hamilton; and Utica, New York State.

The mark on these pieces includes the words T. GODWIN WHARF. The 'wharf' stands for Burslem Wharf, the site of Godwin's Canal Works Pottery.

34 (above left) Knottingley Pottery
Elephant Pattern (A)
(Courtesy: Mr and Mrs Martin Pulver)
Indented plate (1796-1801), in dark blue, with a line-engraved Chinese scene in which the central feature is an elephant with howdah. There are many other figures including a woman riding side-saddle on a horse. The picture is framed in a band of geometrical motifs and the border, from which it is separated, combines the same motif with eight insects and a dagger edge.
Impressed mark: WEDGWOOD & CO near the edge of the base. Also a small incised circle in the centre.
Diam 24.8cm (9.8in). No foot rim. Very pale greenish-blue rippled glaze of fine quality.

35 (above right) Ferrybridge Pottery
Greek Altar Pattern (A)
(Courtesy: Robin Gurnett, Esq)
Indented plate (c 1810-26), in medium blue, with a classical scene of a woman making a sacrifice at an altar with a second woman on her knees playing pipes. Two wreaths or garlands hang from a tree behind them. The scene has a line-engraved net background. The border has eight panels alternating with eagles and pairs of putti against a line-engraved ground.
Impressed mark: FERRYBRIDGE
Diam 22.5cm (8.9in). No foot rim. Slightly rippled blue glaze, a little 'gritty' in places.

36 (below) Thomas Godwin 'American Views'
'Boston and Bunkers Hill'
Dish (c 1840-50), in medium blue, with a view of Boston and Bunkers Hill. The floral border of morning glory and nasturtiums is separated by an unprinted area from the central view.
Printed mark: A pseudo-Royal Arms with an oval shield with inner escutcheon and lion and unicorn supporters. Around the shield are the words 'AMERICAN VIEWS'. A ribbon beneath carries the words OPAQUE CHINA and T. GODWIN WHARF. Below the arms in cursive lettering is the title 'Boston and Bunkers Hill'.
Length 38.9cm (15.3in). Width 30.9cm (12.3in). No foot rim. Smooth colourless glaze.

Goodwin, Bridgwood & Orton of Lane End

This was one of a series of partnerships involving the name Goodwin. There was firstly Goodwin & Orton, then Goodwin & Co, which in 1827 became Goodwin, Bridgwood & Orton of High Street, Lane End. Their wares are not very common, nor are they particularly well potted or printed. The illustrated example (37) bears a printed mark in which the initial letters of the partnership are included—G.B.O.

Goodwins & Harris of Lane End

A new partnership succeeded the two year partnership of Goodwin, Bridgwood & Orton in 1829. This was Goodwin, Bridgwood and Harris which also lasted only two years and was succeeded by Goodwins & Harris. Godden gives the address of this firm as Crown Works, Lane End. It lasted from 1831 to 1838 and was noted for making children's plates. The example (38) impressed with the mark GOODWINS & HARRIS may well have been intended for this purpose.

Charles Harvey & Sons of Longton

John and Charles Harvey are said to have established a pottery at Stafford Street, Longton, at the end of the eighteenth century but John Harvey appears to have left the firm shortly afterwards. Charles Harvey, however, was soon working potteries on other sites in Longton in addition to the Stafford Street works, including one in Great Charles Street, Lane End. The history of the firm is obscure but we do know that Harvey had two sons, Charles and W. K. who continued potting after their father had left the industry. The partnership of Charles Harvey & Sons operated from about 1818 until 1835 when it became C. & W. K. Harvey but the father may well have had only a financial interest in the firm for some years before 1835.

The dish (39) with the view of Edinburgh which is impressed HARVEY would appear to have been made between about 1820 and 1830 though G. A. Godden (GM1967) gives this mark as that of C. & W. K. Harvey (1835-53). It seems likely, however, that it was also used by Charles Harvey & Sons before 1835. A number of other views were included in this series. Alan Smith in his *Liverpool Herculaneum Pottery* (1970) illustrates an unmarked bowl with a view of Oxford (plate 168) which can be attributed to Charles Harvey & Sons.

37 (above left) Goodwin, Bridgwood & Orton
'Oriental Flower Garden'
Moulded and gadrooned plate (c 1827-29), in medium blue, with a Chinese scene seen between a large spray of flowers and a decorative urn with flowers, the whole framed in dentil stringing. The scrolled border has a stippled ground near the gadrooned rim. From this border sprays of flowers extend towards the well of the plate.
Printed mark:

Oriental Flower Garden ⎫ *all within a*
G.B.O. ⎬ *scrolled*
⎭ *cartouche.*

Diam 17.4cm (6.8in). Rounded foot rim. Smooth colourless glaze.

38 (above right) Goodwins & Harris
Stylised Flowers Pattern (A)
Plate (c 1831-38) with wavy edge, in medium-dark blue, with a central pattern of stylised flowers and leaves and a wide border (separately applied) in a similar style.
Impressed mark: GOODWINS & HARRIS
Diam 14.6cm (5.7in). Rounded foot rim. Very slightly rippled blue glaze.

39 (below) Charles Harvey & Sons 'Edinburgh'
(Courtesy: Ian Henderson, Esq)
Indented dish (c 1820-30), double printed in medium and dark blue with a distant view of Edinburgh seen across undulating country, with kilted figures in the foreground. The scrolled border on the dished rim is divided into eight panels with alternating floral motifs against a fine-mesh net ground.
Impressed mark: HARVEY
Printed mark: EDINBURGH *on a scrolled ribbon backed by leaves.*
Length 42.4cm (16.7in). Width 33.9cm (13.3in). No foot rim. Slightly rippled blue glaze.

John Heath of Burslem

There were a number of potters named Heath working in Staffordshire in the first half of the nineteenth century and the mark HEATH might have been used by any of them. It is usually associated, however, with John Heath of the Sytch Pottery, Burslem whose dates are given by G. A. Godden as 1809-23. The plate (40) with *The Girl at the Well* pattern would be described by most collectors at once on its face value as 'Spode' for examples with the SPODE mark are fairly common. The impressed mark on this example, however, is HEATH. The pattern is identical with the Spode pattern but is printed in a slightly darker blue and, unlike Spode examples, the plate has a foot rim.

Whiter dates the introduction of this pattern as 1822, only a year before Heath ceased to operate. It is possible that a Staffordshire engraving establishment supplied the design to both factories.

Henshall & Co of Longport

Wares bearing the mark HENSHALL & CO. are rare. Little records a plate with this mark (plate 34) which also carries a printed wreath enclosing the name of a series—'British Views'. The example illustrated here (41) has an overall pattern identical with a pattern used by Herculaneum. Alan Smith in his *Liverpool Herculaneum Pottery* (1970), plate 151, described this as 'possibly 1804' and it is suggested that the Liverpool Pottery found that it did not sell well and that some of the unsaleable stock may have been exported to Spain in 1814 (*ibid*. p 49). Henshall & Co were in existence at the end of the eighteenth century and it is thought that this mark was used early in the nineteenth century during a partnership with Williamson which lasted into the 1820s. The name Henshall then disappears.

It is interesting to note that the partnership of Henshall & Williamson used the Duke Street warehouse of the Liverpool Herculaneum Pottery after 1807 to sell their wares (ibid. pp 55-6), possibly until the partnership ended. Perhaps the two potteries obtained engravings from the same source. If they came from the engraver James Kennedy of Commercial Street, Burslem, the source of some Herculaneum patterns, the date would have been later for this engraving establishment was in business from about 1818 to 1834.

Herculaneum Pottery, Liverpool

The earliest blue-printed wares were produced at

40 (above left) John Heath
'The Girl at the Well' Pattern
Indented plate (c 1822-23), in dark blue, with a picture of a girl filling a ewer from a well. To the right is a tree, to the left a large spray of leaves and flowers. The border of trailing leaves extends to the well of the plate but is separated from the picture by an unprinted area.
Impressed mark: HEATH
Diam 25cm (9.9in). Double foot rim, the inner part rounded. Rippled blue glaze.

41 (above right) Henshall & Co
'Flowers and Leaves' Pattern
Indented plate (c 1805-25) in medium to dark blue, with an all-over pattern of flowers and leaves within a narrow band of stringing around the rim.
Impressed mark: HENSHALL & CO
Diam 24.1cm (9.5in). No foot rim. Colourless rippled glaze.

42 (below) Herculaneum Pottery
India Patterns (A)
Mausoleum of Nawaub Assoph Khan, Rajmahal Indented dish (c 1809-20), in medium blue, with an Indian scene with a domed building as the central feature. Two figures with camels occupy the foreground and in the background is a peak surmounted by a structure flying a pennant. The border, which is separated from the picture by a narrow unprinted area, is of sea shells, sprays of flowers and small coastal or river scenes, all on a stipple ground.
Impressed mark: HERCULANEUM *in letters under 0.2cm high (GM2007)*
Length 50.8cm (20in). Width 40.6cm (16.4in). No foot rim. Cream coloured body. Pale blue rippled glaze.

this pottery in the 1790s but the main period of production of these wares was from c 1805 to 1830. The earlier wares are of very fine quality, particularly the India patterns which appear to have been launched between c 1809 and 1820. These scenes were derived from T. and W. Daniell's *Oriental Scenery and Views in Hindoostan* published by Robert Bowyer of Pall Mall between 1795 and 1807.

The *View in the Fort of Madura* (43) with its floral border appears to have been a popular one. Alan Smith illustrates a meat dish and plate from a dinner service, a frog mug and a bed pan with this pattern, the mug having a maroon edge (plates 158-9). The impressed mark on the dish illustrated (43) is much larger than that on the dish with the *Mausoleum of Nawaub Assoph Khan* (42).

Several other Herculaneum patterns produced in the 1820s have been recorded including a series of views of towns carrying a border with scrolled medallions and kneeling figures. These include:

Caernarvon Castle (Little, plate 111)
Cambridge (Smith, plate 169)
Shrewsbury (Smith, plate 162)

By 1830 many of the printed wares from the Herculaneum factory were in sepia or black. The author has seen no printed wares in blue which can be identified as having been made at the pottery after it was sold to Case & Mort in 1833.

Hicks, Meigh & Johnson of Shelton

This firm succeeded Hicks and Meigh in 1822, a pottery which had been making stone china for many years. The tureen (44) is a typical example of their dinner wares, printed in a paler blue than most wares of the period. There is some slight doubt as to which partnership made this example which carries the octagonal mark enclosing a crown and the words STONE CHINA. This may also have been used prior to 1822 by Hicks & Meigh. Most of the Hicks, Meigh & Johnson designs are floral (see also Coysh, plates 51 and 52). They do not appear to have favoured scenic patterns. The plate (45) has the rare mark of *H.M.J.*

G. A. Godden states that Hicks, Meigh & Johnson employed some six hundred work people in 1833. (*Mason's Patent Ironstone China* 1971, p 72).

In 1836 the firm was succeeded by Ridgway, Morley, Wear & Co (see pp 64-5) which in 1842 became Ridgway & Morley.

43 (above) Herculaneum Pottery
India Patterns (A)
View in the Fort of Madura
Indented plate (c 1809-20), in medium to dark blue, with an Indian scene in which an elephant carrying two men in a howdah is driven towards a sacred building. In the background is a river or lake with sailing vessels and a mountain peak surmounted by a building.
Impressed mark: HERCULANEUM *in letters 0.3cm high with a '12'*
Length 32.9cm (13in). Width 25.9cm (10.2in). No foot rim. Pale blue-green rippled glaze.

44 (below) Hicks, Meigh & Johnson
Exotic Bird Pattern (A)
(Courtesy: Mr and Mrs S. Henrywood)
Tureen (c 1822-35) in light-medium blue, with a floral pattern in the Chinese taste with exotic birds. The border is of scrolls and geometrical motifs.
Printed mark: A crown with the word STONE *above and* CHINA *below all enclosed within an octagon decorated with ribbons and leaves. Below the octagon 'No. 2' (GM2023)*
Length 29.2cm (11.5in). Width at widest point 19.1cm (7.5in). Height 16.9cm (6.65in). Smooth colourless glaze. The pineapple finial is gilded over the blue glaze.

Indented moulded plate (c 1822-35), in light-medium blue, with a design including many types of fruit— apple, pear, cherry, currant etc. These are combined with sprays of flowers.
Printed mark: a cornucopia below which are the words 'Fruit and Flowers' and below this again H.M.J. Diam 24cm (9.5in). Prominent rounded foot rim. Colourless glaze. The rim has moulded gadrooning.

Jones & Son of Hanley

The British History Series produced by the short-lived Hanley firm of Jones & Son (c 1826-28) is unique and is probably the only series of blue-printed patterns made by this pottery.

The plate (46) shows the *Signing of the Magna Charta at Runnymede* on 15 June 1215. The Great Charter which forms the cornerstone of British liberty and rights was written in Latin and contained articles concerning the Church, Feudalism, Justice and Trade. Perhaps the most important was the decree that no free man was 'to be imprisoned, punished, or outlawed except by the judgment of his equals, or by the law of the land.' One plate with this Magna Charta scene has been noted with the impressed mark 'Jones Superior Staffordshire Ware'.

The tureen stand (47) is of particular interest because it bears the wrong title in the printed mark. The scene shows *The Seven Bishops conveyed to the Tower* but owing to an error the transferrer used the title *'Canute Reproving Courtiers'*. This title, however, adds one more to the list of recorded patterns which now stands at fourteen (Coysh, p 44).

The seven bishops were Sancroft, Archbishop of Canterbury; Lake of Chichester; White of Peterborough, Turner of Ely; Ken of Bath and Wells; Lloyd of St Asaph, and Trelawney of Bristol. When James II issued a second Declaration of Indulgence in 1688 he ordered that it should be read in all churches on two successive Sundays. The Archbishop of Canterbury with the six other Bishops asked to be excused from reading the document. James was angry and ordered that they should be committed to the Tower. They were taken by boat on the Thames followed by boats full of supporters. In due course the Bishops were tried and at the end of the hearing were acquitted. There was almost universal rejoicing. James had alienated the country. Before the end of the year William of Orange had landed at Torbay and James II was in flight.

46 (above right) Jones & Son
'British History' Series
'Signing of the Magna Charta'
(Courtesy Mrs Elizabeth Carter)
Plate with wavy edge and four cusps (c 1826-28). In medium and dark blue, with a scene showing King John being presented with the Magna Charta by three barons in the presence of two bishops. The border has alternate motifs showing respectively a crown and mitre, with rose, thistle and shamrock, and a group of military and naval accoutrements.
Printed mark: Britannia and the seated figure of a woman to right and left of a gothic archway surmounted by a crown. Below the crown are the words BRITISH HISTORY. On a tablet beneath the archway is the name of the maker—JONES & SON. Within the archway is the name of the scene—SIGNING OF MAGNA CHARTA.
Diam 25cm (9.3in). Single foot rim, Slightly rippled blue glaze on white body.

47 (below) Jones & Son   *'British History Series'*
'The Seven Bishops conveyed to the Tower'
Tureen stand with wavy edge and four cusps (c 1826-28), in medium and dark blue, with a scene showing the seven bishops being conveyed to the tower. Two soldiers stand guard while the bishops embark in a boat on the Thames held by three boatmen. A woman and child express sympathy for the bishops. The border is as in 46 (above). The handles are covered in a dark blue translucent glaze.
Printed mark: as in 46 above except that the title reads—CANUTE REPROVING HIS COURTIERS. (This is an error on the part of the transferrer). The correct title is THE SEVEN BISHOPS CONVEYED TO THE TOWER.
Length 39.6cm (15.4in). Width 26.5cm (10.4in). No foot rim. Slightly rippled pale blue glaze.

Leeds Old Pottery

The single word 'Leeds' is often used to describe earthenwares from this city. There were, in fact, thirty potteries working in Leeds in the first half of the nineteenth century so it is important to attribute wares to a single pottery since, although many of them made only stonewares and terra cotta, several also produced creamwares and at least two produced blue-printed wares. The Leeds Old Pottery in Jack Lane, Hunslett, was, however, the most important, particularly during the partnership of Hartley, Greens & Co between 1781 and 1822. This was the period when blue-printed wares were made, mainly towards the end of the partnership.

Relatively few blue-printed patterns from Leeds Old Pottery have been recorded. Large quantities of a two-man willow pattern (Coysh, plate 12) were made, a classical scene after Claude Lorraine (Coysh, plate 55), a countryside scene with men and horses which has a border containing passion flowers (Little, plate 98), and a parrot and fruit design (Little, plate 96). It is now possible to add two more to the list. *The Wanderer Pattern* (48 a and b), as is usual with Leeds Old Pottery, has an earthenware body which is thinly potted and very light in weight. The plate weighs only a fraction over six ounces, two ounces lighter than the average for plates of the same diameter. The large dish (49) is heavier and carries a pattern with pagodas and a wall climbing the hill behind them—obviously intended to represent the *Great Wall of China*. It is well printed and has a particularly fine glaze.

The other Leeds firm producing blue-printed wares was Petty's Pottery which operated under several partnerships including the name of Petty from 1792 to 1847 (see pp 54-5). A. Hurst in his *Catalogue of the Boynton Collection of Yorkshire Pottery* (1922) warns of the danger of attributing unmarked wares from this factory to Leeds Old Pottery.

48 (above left) Leeds Old Pottery
The Wanderer Pattern (A)
Plate (c 1810-20), in medium to dark blue, with a country scene with cottage, church and river. A man carrying a bundle on a crooked stick is calling a dog. The border is a folded ribbon against a 'vermicelli' background and the space between the border and the central picture is printed with 'vermicelli'.
Impressed mark: HARTLEY GREENS & CO.
LEEDS POTTERY
arranged in a semi-circle.
Diam 18.3cm (7.4in). Single foot rim. Rippled blue glaze.

48a (above right) Leeds Old Pottery
The Wanderer Pattern (A)
(Courtesy: Mrs Elizabeth Carter)
Coffee pot (c 1810-20), in medium to dark blue, with pattern and border as on 48. The border pattern also decorates the handle and the spout (chipped) is decorated with sprays of flowers.
Impressed mark: HARTLEY GREENS & CO.
LEEDS POTTERY
Height to rim: 20.3cm (8in). Diam of base 9.9cm (3.8in). The spout of the pot has a triangular strainer with 17 perforations. Rounded foot rim. Smooth blue glaze on pale cream body.

49 (below) Leeds Old Pottery
The Great Wall of China Pattern (A)
Indented dish (c 1800-1810) in medium blue, with a Chinese scene showing the Great Wall of China between two 3-storey pagodas. In the foreground are fields with rows of crops through which a river flows on which there is a sampan with sail. A man on the river bank smokes a pipe and is fishing. A second man is seated watching a dog. Two large palm trees with fruit provide prominent features. The scene is framed in a band with a cellular motif broken in four places by stylised flowers. The border is of geometrical motifs, scrolls and flowers.
Impressed mark: LEEDS POTTERY
Length 45.7cm (18.4in). Width 34.3cm (13.5in). A high foot rim raises one end of the dish so that meat juices can drain down shallow channels to a gravy well at the other end. Rippled blue glaze.

The Mason Family of Lane End

Miles Mason who started potting in Liverpool c 1792 had previously run a business in London importing Chinese porcelain. While he was in London his eldest son, William, was born in 1785. When Miles Mason moved to Staffordshire in 1800 William was 15 years of age and shortly afterwards is said to have joined his father, moving to the Minerva Works at Lane Delph in 1806. His name is directly associated with the firm in 1814 soon after his father's retirement and there are two recorded examples of blue-printed wares bearing the mark W. MASON. One of these is illustrated by G. A. Godden (GI389) and the comport (50 a and b) bears the same pattern as this example and may be attributed to the same maker though the borders differ slightly: one includes a convolvulus flower but this is omitted from the border of the comport, possibly for convenience in adapting it to a smaller shape. Andrew Stevenson produced a view of gothic ruins (Coysh, plate 124) which has much in common with this Mason example. Indeed, one asks whether the rare W. MASON mark may have been a retailer's mark for William Mason's main business appears to have been in the retail trade at Smithy Door in Manchester though he is known to have taken a pottery at Fenton Culvert for a short period in 1822.

The most important Mason firm for blue printed wares was that of G. M. & C. J. Mason. George and Charles were two younger sons of Miles Mason who took over from their father when he retired and established the Patent Ironstone Manufactory at Lane Delph. 'Mason's Patent Ironstone China' was introduced in 1813. Although most of the dinner wares using this body were decorated in several colours, a considerable output was blue-printed. A number of patterns have already been illustrated (Coysh, plates 57-9). Two more are now recorded. They have been tentatively named the *Two-man Chinoiserie Pattern* (53) and *Oriental Panel Pattern* (54). Collectors should be careful to discriminate between the early wares and those made by the successors of G. M. & C. J. Mason. From 1813 to 1825 the wares were normally impressed with the words MASON'S PATENT IRONSTONE CHINA printed in a straight line, or occasionally in two lines. The printed marks are less reliable. These have been used with variations over a long period by succeeding companies—C. J. Mason & Co (1829-45), Francis Morley & Co (1845-58), and G. L. Ashworth (1862-present day). A full account

Note. View page 67 from outer edge.

50a (above left) Attributed to William Mason
Ruined Abbey Pattern (A)
(Courtesy: Mrs Elizabeth Carter)
The inside of a comport (c 1811-24), seen from above, printed in dark medium blue with a scene of a ruined abbey in hilly country. There are deer and figures in the foreground. The border consists of four little scenes with cottages in elaborately scrolled medallions separated by sprays of leaves and flowers against a stipple ground. The handles are covered with a cobalt wash (underglaze)
Length 33.8cm (13.3in). Width 23.6cm (9.3in).

50b (above right)
Comport (c 1811-24), in elevation, printed in dark medium blue, with a country scene with lake and sailing boat. In the distance are hills and ruins.
Printed mark: Small blue triangle on recessed base.
Height to handle 13cm (5.1in). Blue glaze on white body.

51 (below left) Attributed to C. J. Mason & Co
The Fountain Pattern (A)
(Courtesy: Robin Gurnett, Esq)
Moulded dish with wavy edge (c 1826-30), in medium blue, with a parkland scene with figures. There is a large country mansion and an elaborate fountain in the foreground with Hercules attacking the Lernean hydra. Deer rest beneath a tree. The border of flowers and leaves on a stipple ground is broken by cusped motifs which point inwards.
Printed mark: SEMI-CHINA
WARRANTED
Length 28.5cm (11.2in). Flattened foot rim. Rippled blue glaze on white body.

52 (below right) Attributed to C. J. Mason & Co
'Chinese Dragon' Pattern
(Courtesy: Robin Gurnett, Esq)
Moulded dish with wavy edge (c 1826-30), in medium blue, with a single Chinese dragon. The border carries a speckled serpent and various scroll motifs with the same scale-shading as the dragon's body.
Impressed mark: MASON'S CAMBRIAN ARGIL
Length 28.5cm (11.2in). Flattened foot rim. Colourless rippled on cream-coloured body.

of the development of Mason's Ironstone and the marks used by the firm is given in G. A. Godden's *Mason's Patent Ironstone China* (1971).

C. J. Mason & Co

In 1826 the partnership of G. M. & C. J. Mason ended and the firm became C. J. Mason & Co. It continued to produce ironstone services but appears to have introduced two new bodies—'Bandana' ware and 'Mason's Cambrian Argil' which were used for their blue-printed ware output. 'Argil' is the name for potter's clay and this may well have come from Wales or, more likely, from Cornwall via the Cambrian Pottery in Swansea which imported clay from the south-west of England. The patterns on the two moulded dishes (51 and 52) have already been illustrated (Coysh, plates 58 and 146.) They are shown here side by side on identical shapes, one bearing the MASON'S CAMBRIAN ARGIL mark (52). This suggests that the *Fountain Pattern* (51) may also be a Mason product. It bears the printed words SEMI-CHINA WARRANTED which G. A. Godden records as a mark found on Mason wares (see *Mason's Patent Ironstone China*, 1971, p 45). A plate with the *Fountain Pattern* has also been noted with the mark BRITISH NAN-KEEN CHINA a description used by Miles Mason from 1805 which almost certainly continued when his sons took over.

A plate with the *Fountain Pattern* (Coysh, plate 146) has the printed mark HIGGINBOTHAM'S SEMI-CHINA WARRANTED. This is the name of a Dublin retailer. A collector has reported an ironstone plate with: THOMAS & HIGGIN-BOTHAM, 11-12 Wellington Quay, Dublin on the base and another collector has found the base of an earthenware bowl on the river bank at Coalport with a blue-printed mark 'HIGGINBOTHAM & Co., Grafton Street, Dublin'.

Robert May of Hanley

Robert May was in the partnership of Toft and May in Hanley from about 1825 until 1829 when the firm was operated by Robert May alone. A year later it was taken over by William Ridgway. The plate with the *Bird Fountain Pattern* has the rare impressed mark—MAY. This appears to be the only example so far recorded.

53 (*above left*) *G. M. & C. J. Mason*
Two-man Chinoisierie Pattern (A)
(*Courtesy: Robin Gurnett, Esq*)
Indented plate (1813-25), in medium blue, with a Chinese scene of two figures and two birds. The border of Chinese motifs is restricted to the rim. Impressed mark:
MASON'S PATENT IRONSTONE CHINA *in one line (GM2539)*
Diam 23.7cm (9.4in). Narrow double foot rim. Greenish-blue glaze on ironstone. Weight 1 lb 3½ oz.

54 (*above right*) *G. M. & C. J. Mason*
Oriental Panel Pattern (A)
(*Courtesy: Robin Gurnett, Esq*)
Indented plate (1813-25) with an overall pattern in medium blue, six oriental panels include three circular panels of stylised flowers and geometrical motifs and three panels of irregular shape with trees, birds or animals. The panels are on a dark background with stylised flowers in white.
Printed mark: MASON'S *above a crown and drape which carries the words* PATENT IRONSTONE CHINA *(GM2530)*
Impressed mark: as in 53 above.
Diam 24cm (9.5in). Narrow double foot rim. Thick white glaze on ironstone which shows light brown where glaze is chipped. Weight 1 lb 2 oz.

55 (*below left*) *attributed to C. J. Mason & Co.*
Classical Landscape Pattern (A)
Indented plate (c 1826-30) in medium blue, with classical landscape with ruins, within an octagonal frame. The scene includes a man on horseback and a lake with a boat. The border consists of fragments of pillars, capitals and entablatures with an acanthus stringing on the edge of the rim.
Impressed mark: MASON'S CAMBRIAN ARGIL
Diam 24.8cm (9.2in). No foot rim. Colourless rippled glaze.

56 (*below right*) *Robert May*
The Bird Fountain Pattern (A)
(*Courtesy: Robin Gurnett, Esq*)
Plate (c 1830), double-printed in light and dark violet-blue, with a parkland scene with river, bridge and classical buildings. A prominent feature is a fountain, the upper part supported by two long-necked birds, the lower by two dolphins. A man, woman and small girl walk in the park with a dog.
Impressed mark: MAY
Diam 24.2cm (9.5in). No foot rim. Colourless glaze.

John Meir of Tunstall

The early wares of John Meir's pottery at Tunstall made between about 1812 and 1820 were of particularly high quality. The *River Fishing Pattern* (Coysh, plate 61) is a good example. When he took over the Greengates Pottery from Benjamin Adam c 1820 the quality seems to have started to fall off a little. The pattern on the moulded punch bowl (57) is entitled *Byron's Illustrations* and dates from early in the 1830s. There was a great interest in Byron's romantic writing in his day and for some years after his death. He was considered to be the greatest English poet and he had a high reputation abroad. The illustrations in his works were carried out by two brilliant engravers—William Finden (1787-1852) and his younger brother Edward Francis Finden (1792-1857). These were published in three volumes as *Landscape Illustrations to the Life and Works of Lord Byron* between 1831 and 1834 and there is little doubt that Meir based his blue-printed series on these engravings, either before, or more probably after, they were collected together and published in this new form.

In 1837 John Meir took his son into partnership and the firm became John Meir & Son.

It is worth noting here that between 1831 and 1838 Goodwins & Harris of Lane End produced dinner services printed in brown with scenes relating to Byron's poems with the appropriate quotations from the poems printed on the back of the plates and dishes.

57a (above) John Meir 'Byron's Illustrations' Series 'Simplon' Pattern
(*Courtesy: Mrs Elizabeth Carter*)
Punch bowl (c 1830), in medium blue, viewed from above. The surface is smooth and printed with an Alpine scene in the Simplon Pass showing a village with the Alps rising behind it. In the foreground a man accompanies a child riding on a mule or donkey. The scene is framed in a border pattern of medallions with flowers and birds.
Printed mark: I.M. *within a cartouche of C-scrolls and flowers. Above the cartouche are the words.*

BYRON'S ILLUSTRATIONS
Below the cartouche is the word:
SIMPLON

Diam 29.7cm (11.7in). Height to rim 13cm (5.1in). Blue glaze on white body.
57b (below)
Punch bowl (as above) seen in elevation. The exterior is moulded with loops of diamond shaped beading and printed with the same border of medallions with flowers and birds which decorates the inside.

John Meir & Son of Tunstall

When John Meir took his son into partnership in 1837 the firm used the mark J. M. & S. or I. M. & S. on their blue-printed wares. J. M. & S. was also used by Job Meigh & Son of the Old Hall Pottery, Hanley, another maker of blue-printed wares (Coysh, pp 46-7). However, the mark on the three examples of Northern Scenery (58, 59 and 60) is I.M.S. and there is little doubt that this was the mark of John Meir & Son since there are two similar plates in the Godden Collection one of which bears the full name of John Meir & Son and the other I.M.S. (GM p 431).

The *Northern Scenery* series is well potted with a white body and good quality smooth glaze. The examples of these named views so far recorded are all from the Scottish counties of Argyllshire, Inverness, Lanarkshire, Perthshire and Stirling. These include:

Loch Achray
Loch Awe
Bothwell Castle
Loch Creran with Barcaldine Castle
Dunolly Castle, near Oban
Inverness
Loch Katrine looking towards Ellens Isle
Kilchurn Castle, Loch Awe
Loch Leven looking towards Ballachulish Ferry
Loch Oich and Invergarry Castle
Pass of the Trossachs, Loch Katrine

The names of individual scenes on the printed marks are often difficult to decipher: clearly they were engraved in script by someone quite unfamiliar with Scottish names.

The works of John Meir & Son continued until 1897. Care should be taken to distinguish between early wares and those of late Victorian times when the quality had declined.

58 (above left) Attributed to John Meir & Son
'Northern Scenery' Series
'Loch Creran and Barcaldine Castle'
Covered jug (c 1837-50), in medium blue, with a view of Loch Creran on which there are several sailing boats. Barcaldine Castle is seen in the foreground and in the distance is a complex of high peaks. The border is of flowers, C-scrolls and geometrical motifs. Printed mark: An oval strap with lion and unicorn supporters. Within the oval which is surmounted by a crown are the words NORTHERN SCENERY. On a ribbon beneath are the letters I.M. & S and beneath this is the title of the pattern—'Loch Creran and Barcaldine Castle' in flowing script.
Height to top of lid knop 16.8cm (6.6in). The neck has a 15-hole strainer behind the spout. Smooth pale blue glaze on white body.

59 (above right) Attributed to John Meir & Son
'Northern Scenery' Series
'Dunolly Castle near Oban'
(Courtesy: Ian Henderson, Esq)
Mug (c 1837-50), in medium blue, with a view of Dunolly Castle near Oban. The scene is of mountainous country with lakes on which there are sailing boats. Border as in 58 above.
Printed mark: as in 58 above except that the title of the pattern is 'Dunolly Castle near Oban'.
Height 12.5cm (4.9in). Diameter of splayed base 13.1cm (5.1in). Foot rim. Smooth pale blue glaze on white body.

60 (below) Attributed to John Meir & Son
'Northern Scenery' Series
'Loch Awe'
(Courtesy: Ian Henderson, Esq)
Indented dish (c 1837-50), in medium blue, with a view of Loch Awe. There are sailing ships on the lake and mountains in the distance. Border as in 58 above which descends to the well of the dish.
Printed mark: as in 58 above except that the title of the pattern is 'Loch Awe'.
Length 39.6cm (15.6in). Width 34.3cm (13.5in). No foot rim. Smooth colourless glaze on white body.

Mintons of Stoke

The output of earthenwares from the Minton factory at Stoke has always been considerable. Since few pieces were marked in the years from 1796 to 1823 it is difficult to identify the early wares. A summary of the firm's history gives perspective:

1793   Thomas Minton (1765-1836) established a pot works at Stoke in partnership with Joseph Poulson.

1796   Blue-printed wares made for the first time to be sold mainly through the London agency of Arthur Minton, Thomas Minton's brother.

1806   Poulson appears to have left the firm.

1817   Thomas Minton took his sons, Thomas and Herbert, into partnership to form the firm Thomas Minton & Sons.

1823   Thomas Minton Jr left and the partnership was dissolved. The factory began to mark its earthenwares with an *M*.

1836   Death of Thomas Minton Sr. Herbert Minton took over the management and late in the year formed a partnership with John Boyle (*M. & B.*)

1841   The Minton & Boyle partnership ended. Herbert Minton took his nephew Michael Daintry Hollins into partnership. The firm was known as Herbert Minton & Co and continued to use this name after 1849 when another nephew, Colin Minton Campbell became the third partner. From 1841 the mark was mainly M. & Co. though after 1845 the mark *M. & H.* was sometimes used.

The tureen (61) with the *Genevese Pattern* was made between 1830 and 1836. The shape corresponds to 'D' in the factory shape book used in the 1830-40 period (See G. A. Godden, *Minton Pottery and Porcelain of the First Period 1793-1850*. 1968. Plate 46) and the mark indicates a date before the Minton & Boyle partnership. The pattern has been freely adapted to fit the various surfaces. The appearance of the *Genevese Pattern* on unmarked wares should not be taken to indicate a Minton origin. The pattern was also used by other potters— Thomas & Benjamin Godwin, for example.

The Swiss Cottage Pattern (62) and the Minton & Boyle *Devon Pattern* (63) are typical of their period. These patterns were designed for the purpose, not adapted from book illustrations. They leave considerable areas of the fine white body, known by the Minton firm as 'Opaque China', without printing so that the overall impression is one of lightness.

61 (above) Minton of Stoke   'Genevese' Pattern Tureen (c 1830-36), in medium blue, with Alpine scenes of chalets, lakes and mountains with foregrounds of flowers and C-scrolls. The patterns on the lid and the sides differ from that inside the tureen but are similar in style. There is a border of flowers and C-scrolls on the lid and inside the rim. The handles and feet are moulded with scroll-motifs.
Printed mark: 'Genevese' *within a scroll and flower cartouche. Below the cartouche:*
                Opaque M China
Overall length 38.1cm (15in). Overall height 27.4cm (10.8in). Fine colourless glaze on smooth white body.

62 (below left) Minton of Stoke   'Swiss Cottage' Pattern Saucer dish (c 1830-36), in medium blue, with a rural scene dominated by a chalet to which a path leads by way of a five-barred gate. A deep border to the dish is of flowers and scrolls inset with small views of buildings.
Printed mark: SWISS COTTAGE *on a scroll above an 'M' in script. Beneath this is a second scroll with the words 'Opaque China', also in script.*
Diam 21.6cm (8.5in). Height above rounded foot rim 4.6cm (1.8in). Smooth colourless glaze.

63 (below right) Minton & Boyle   'Devon' Pattern (Courtesy: Ian Henderson, Esq)
Plate with wavy edge (1836-41), in light violet-blue, with a rural scene showing a church and two men fishing in a lake or river. The wide border which extends to the well of the plate has alternate sprays of flowers, including convolvulus and flowing acanthus-style leaves, all against a background of folded drapery edged with scrolls.
Impressed mark: 'IMPROVED STONE STONA' *within an eight-sided panel.*
Printed mark: 'DEVON' *within a cartouche (GM 2693) below which are the letters* M & B.
Diam 26.2cm (10.3in). Double foot rim. Smooth clear glaze on white body.

Samuel Moore & Co of Sunderland

At the end of the eighteenth century a number of potteries were already well established near the estuary of the River Wear and they grew in importance during the first half of the nineteenth century. At least two produced blue-printed earthenwares—the Garrison Pottery at Sunderland and the Wear Pottery at Southwick. Examples from the Garrison Pottery with the mark of Dixon, Austin & Co (1820-26) have been recorded in J. T. Shaw's *The Potteries of Sunderland and District* (Third Edition, 1968. Plate 7).

The tea bowl and saucer with the *Gazelle Pattern* (64) bears the mark on the saucer of S. Moore & Co of the Wear Pottery, Sunderland. This was operated from 1803 by the partnership of Samuel Moore and Peter Austin but both partners had other interests and in the 1830s the actual management passed to Charles Moore though the firm continued to trade as S. Moore & Co until 1861. These tewares are very thinly potted and the printing is in a very deep blue. It is difficult to date them accurately but they must have been made between about 1820 and 1840.

Francis Morley & Co of Shelton, Hanley

The factory operated by Francis Morley & Co from 1844 until 1858 originally belonged to Hicks, Meigh & Johnson until 1836, then became Ridgway, Morley, Wear & Co until 1842 and for the next two years Ridgway & Morley. All these firms produced stone china and Francis Morley obtained the designs of the Mason Ironstone China from C. J. Mason in 1848. The *American Marine Pattern* (65) was made for export and proved very popular. It was, however, produced by G. L. Ashworth Bros at a much later date—even as late as the 1950s.

Petty's Pottery, Leeds

Petty's Pottery, sometimes known as Hunslet Hall, was established in the eighteenth century and was operated in 1792 by Rainforth & Co. Some impressed marks show this form. The firm was second only to the Leeds Old Pottery of Hartley, Greens & Co among the many potteries in the city and exported similar wares, mainly to Brazil. In 1818 it became Petty's & Co, in 1822 Petty & Hewitt and in 1825 Samuel Petty & Son. Blue-printed wares were made in the Rainforth period and also when the firm became Pettys & Co (66).

64 (above) Samuel Moore & Co 'Gazelle' Pattern Tea bowl and saucer (c 1820-40) printed in very dark blue, with a pattern showing a girl seated with a gazelle against a lattice background with leaves and flowers. The separate border has quatrefoil floral medallions linked by swags against a lattice background which extends to the rim inside the cup and on the saucer.
Impressed mark on saucer: MOORE
Printed mark on saucer: GAZELLE in a C-scroll cartouche beneath which is the maker's name—S. MOORE & CO. The footrim of the bowl is vertical on the outside and slopes inwards on the inside. The foot rim of the saucer is rounded.
Diam of saucer 17.7cm (5in). Diam of bowl 7.6cm (3in). Blue glaze on thinly potted lightweight body: the bowl weighs less than 2 oz.

65 (below left) Francis Morley & Co
'American Marine' Pattern
Indented plate (1845-50), in medium blue, with a seascape with fishing boats. The border has four panels outlined in a rope-motif each with a scene with sailing boats and paddle steamers.
Printed mark: A sailing boat with AMERICAN MARINE on a ribbon beneath, and the initals F. M. & CO.
Diam 22.3cm (9in). Rounded foot rim. Clear colourless glaze.

66 (below right) Pettys & Co Gazebo Pattern (A) (Courtesy: Robin Gurnett, Esq)
Indented plate (1818-22) in medium blue, with a rural scene with country house, a gazebo and church. Cattle are prominent in the foreground. A wide floral border on a stipple ground includes passion flowers and extends to the well of the plate, where it is separated from the central scene by stringing.
Impressed mark: PETTYS & CO. LEEDS
Diam 24.6cm (9.7in). Thickly potted with a double foot rim and pale blue 'gritty' glaze.

Edward & George Phillips of Longport

The partnership of Edward & George Phillips is known to have existed in 1822 but one or both of the partners must have been a potter with considerable experience. It continued for twelve years and built up a prosperous trade with America. Indeed, their wares seem to be commoner in that country than in Britain. N. Hudson Moore in *The Old China Book* (1903) illustrated a cup and saucer made by E. & G. Phillip with a print of Franklin's Tomb. Wares were also exported with the view of Eton College (69) and also wares with floral designs under the general series title 'British Flowers'. Moore states that 'the designs on the face . . . are graceful bunches of fruit and flowers, distinguished by the same careful printing, and true blue which we notice on the other Phillips designs'.

L. Jewitt in his Ceramic *Art of Great Britain* (1883) refers to James Edwards who as manager of E. & G. Phillips must have contributed greatly to their success. 'James Edwards was an entirely self-made man, and was one of those bright examples of indomitable perseverence, unflinching rectitude, steadiness of purpose and genuine benevolence which crop up now and then among our most successful manufacturers'. Commencing as a thrower at Messrs. Rogers he became a manager at Phillips of Longport, and at Alcock's of Cobridge. By 1842 Edwards was able to buy the Dale Hall Works at Burslem which he later operated with his son.

The coffee pot (67) with the *Guitar Pattern* is remarkably well made with a good white body and fine smooth glaze. The design is highly original, almost pretentious.

The moulded plate (68) also departs from the common shape with an elaborate indented and serpentine rim with moulding. The printed pattern is typical of the period but has an unusual feature. The border owes something to the Spode filigree pattern (Coysh, plate 121) but has been printed in a darker blue *over* the frame of the central design to enclose flower sprays in six separate panels. The base has an unusual triple foot rim. These wares usually carry the name of the pattern in a cartouche of C-scrolls and flowers with the name of the firm beneath—E. & G. PHILLIPS.

67 Edward & George Phillips   *'Guitar' Pattern*
(Courtesy: Robin Gurnett, Esq)
Coffee pot (1822-34), in medium blue, with the title pattern on the spout of a man standing and playing a guitar against a background of a lake and a cottage The pattern around the pot consists of five bands of scrolls and flowers with groups of musical instruments in which a drum is prominent. The three upper bands are inverted. The same motifs are printed on knop and the handle which consists of a large C-scroll supported on a second elongated scroll.
Printed mark: GUITAR in a cartouche outlined by two facing C-scrolls. Beneath this is the maker's name—E. & G. PHILLIPS.
Overall height 28.4cm (11.2in). Width at recessed base 11.6cm (4.5in). Flattened foot rim. Fifteen-hole strainer to spout. Pierced hole in lid has rough edges. Smooth colourless glaze on white body.

George Phillips of Longport

Edward Phillips left the firm of E. & G. Phillips in 1834 which then became simply George Phillips until 1848. There was, however, some deterioration in the quality of the wares. This was typical of the 1835-1850 period. The middle class market had been saturated and potters had to find ways of cheapening their wares in order to create a new market among the working classes. Wares were more heavily potted, there were fewer original designs and colours other than blue were increasingly used.

The *Eton College Pattern* (69) used on export wares by E. & G. Phillips was continued by George Phillips. It is not safe, however, to assume that unmarked pieces with this pattern were made by this firm. Other Staffordshire potters are known to have used the pattern. The mark of George Phillips seldom includes the initial 'G' but it can usually be recognised by the presence of a Staffordshire knot. The name of the body (e.g. OPAQUE CHINA) is sometimes added on a rock cartouche.

Pountney & Allies of Bristol

Pountney & Allies of the Temple Backs Pottery, Bristol, operated from 1816 until 1836 when Edward Allies retired and a Mr Goldney entered into partnership with John D. Pountney. The output of blue-printed earthenware was considerable during both partnerships. A good deal of toilet ware was made for bedroom use, particularly ewers and basins. The bowls usually have a deep foot rim, seldom more than 18cm (7in) in diameter. This fitted into a circular hole cut in the wooden top of the washstand. In Victorian times marble tops for washstands gradually became popular and the deep foot rims began to disappear in favour of a broader base. The bowl (70) seen from above, is a good example of the earlier period—probably made in the reign of William IV. It has an enormous urn or vase in the foreground (cf *The Seasons* pattern of Copeland and Garrett, p 23), an exotic bird, and sailing ships. Ships often appear on Bristol Pottery wares for, after all, Bristol then vied with London as a port. The quality of printing is very fine and the bowl bears an interesting mark with the pattern title— FANCY VASE as well as the impressed mark POUNTNEY & ALLIES.

68 (above left) Edward & George Phillips
'Chinese Views' Pattern
Dished plate (c 1822-34) with moulded indented and serpentine edge, printed in pale and medium blue. The central scene in pale blue has pagodas and a boat with sail on an estuary. This is framed in a pale blue stipple band with flowers. The main border in darker blue is divided into six panels with sprays of flowers. The intervening areas are decorated with scrolls and flowers against a stipple ground.
Printed mark: CHINESE VIEWS *within a cartouche of C-scrolls, flowers and leaves. Beneath this is the maker's name—*E. & G. PHILLIPS
Diam 26.4cm (10.4in). Treble foot rim. Smooth colourless glaze.

69 (above right) George Phillips
'Eton College' Pattern
(Courtesy: Robin Gurnett, Esq)
Indented dished plate (c 1834-48), double printed in medium and dark blue, with a scene with a sailing boat on a lake, and distant buildings. Prominent in the foreground are a man, woman and child. The border of flowers and scrolls has a stipple ground near the rim but the flowers which extend into the well of the plate have no background.
Impressed mark: PHILLIP'S *and* LONGPORT *respectively above and below a Staffordshire knot.*
Printed mark: OPAQUE CHINA *on a rock cartouche with plants.*
Diam 24.8cm (9.8in). Narrow double foot rim. Deep blue rippled glaze.

70 (below) Pountney & Allies 'Fancy Vase' Pattern
Indented moulded bowl (c 1820-35), in medium blue, with a central pattern dominated by a large vase decorated with classical figures which is filled with flowers. An exotic bird is perched on one spray. The foreground is of flowers and leaves. The background has a stretch of water with islands and sailing ships. A wide border around the bowl both outside and inside carries a scene with sailing ships seen between flowers which rise from a sea-shell vase on one side and a basket on the other. A butterfly adorns the sea-shell vase. This scene is repeated three times on panels separated by stippled areas with a bird on a branch.
Impressed mark: POUNTNEY & ALLIES
Printed mark: P
FANCY
VASE } *on a circular medallion.*
A
Diam at rim 34cm (13.4in). Diam at foot rim 18cm (7.1in). Height 11.4cm (4.5in). Smooth colourless glaze on white body.

The series with *Views near Bristol* produced by the Bristol Pottery are well known. The engravings are particularly fine and were probably specially commissioned or done by the firm's own engraver for it has not been possible to trace any book from which they may have been taken. The dish (71) shows the River Avon with the limestone cliffs of the Avon Gorge on the left. In the foreground is a lime-kiln using the limestone from a local quarry. The picture is double-printed. The river, houses and cliffs have been engraved using stipple for the sky and cliffs and line engraving for the water which shows clear reflections. Over this has been printed the foreground with the tree, the kiln and the two kiln workers with their wheelbarrow. This was a technique used by Rogers in the late 1820s and early 1830s. It has always seemed possible that a skilled worker from this firm may have joined Pountney & Allies bringing the 'Drama' series with him (Coysh, p 52). Perhaps the same recruit introduced this technique to Bristol.

The success of the *Views near Bristol* series no doubt encouraged the firm to look further afield. There is a view of Chepstow Castle on the other side of the Severn and a number of views of places on or near the *River Thames* which seems to have been another series title. Those so far recorded are:

Oxford (72)

Park Place near Henley

Richmond Bridge

A view of Pangbourne noted on a very late vegetable dish (c 1900) made by Pountney & Co with the same cartouche as the Thames Series as well as the later factory mark is no doubt a reproduction of a design in the original series so Pangbourne may reasonably be added to the list.

71 (*above*) *Attributed to Pountney & Allies*
'Views near Bristol' Series
'River Avon' Pattern
Eight-sided indented dish (c 1825-35), double-printed in medium to dark blue, with a scene on the River Avon, Bristol, with sailing ships and rowing boats. The limestone cliffs of the Avon Gorge rise steeply from the river bank and a kiln for burning lime is seen in the foreground. The picture is framed in a stringing of small scrolls and stylised leaves. The border pattern of flowers and swags has a stipple ground and the flowers extend to the well of the dish.
Printed mark: VIEW near BRISTOL
RIVER AVON
within a cartouche of leaves and scrolls.
Length 40.9cm (16.1in). Width 30.2cm (11.9in). No foot rim. Pale blue rippled glaze.

72 (*below*) *Attributed to Pountney & Allies*
'River Thames' Series
'Oxford' Pattern
(*Courtesy: Mrs Elizabeth Carter*)
Tureen (c 1825-35), double printed in light blue and dark blue, with a view of Oxford from the River Thames. A man in academic dress follows a pathway by the riverside and there is a sailing boat on the river. The inverted border pattern around the base of the tureen is of flowers and swags suspended from rings against a stipple ground. Inside the rim of the tureen is a stringing of small scrolls and stylised leaves.
Printed mark: OXFORD
RIVER THAMES
inside a cartouche of leaves and scrolls.
Overall length 36.6cm (14.4in). Overall width 22.4cm (8.8in). Height 16.5cm (6.5in). The recessed base has 17 small stilt marks forming an oval.

John & William Ridgway of Hanley

Seventeen views of Oxford and Cambridge Colleges have already been recorded on Ridgway wares (Coysh, page 54). The view of the fountain at Trinity College, Cambridge, printed inside two moulded baskets, adds one more to the list. This fountain in the centre of the Great Court at Trinity was built in 1602 by Thomas Neville who was Master of Trinity from 1593 to 1615. The conduit which supplies it with water was laid by Franciscan friars to supply their house which was on the site now occupied by Sidney Sussex College. Until the nineteenth century it was the principal water supply for Trinity College. Behind the fountain the print shows the Master's Lodge and the Clock Tower on the north side of the Court which carries a statue of Edward III and an eighteenth century clock.

These baskets (73 and 74) show high quality workmanship. Ridgway used similar moulds on hand-painted porcelain baskets (see Godden G. A. *An Illustrated Encyclopaedia of British Pottery and Porcelain.* 1966. Plate 478). The design may have been taken from Wedgwood wares for two baskets of the same shape, painted in brown and attributed to Wedgwood (c 1769) are to be seen at Knole, Kent, in Lady Betty's china closet.

Although both baskets (73 and 74) are unmarked, there is little doubt about their attributions to John & William Ridgway for many marked specimens in this printed series are known. They are not a matching pair: the handles which have been treated with a dark blue translucent glaze are different and only one of the baskets has decorative moulding between the perforations.

In 1830 the partnership between John & William Ridgway ended. William Ridgway then took over the Bell Works at Shelton, Hanley. The firm became William Ridgway & Co in 1834 and William Ridgway, Son & Co in 1836.

William Ridgway, Son & Co

When Edward J. Ridgway (William Ridgway's son) joined the firm in 1836 the output of blue-printed wares was already declining in favour of green, brown and black. Between about 1843 and 1850 dinner services in green or black carried a series title *Humphrey's Clock* (see GM3309). This was derived from the magazine launched by Charles Dickens under the title of *Master Humphrey's Clock* (1840-1) which serialized *The Old Curiosity Shop* and *Barnaby Rudge*. The illustrator was Hablot Browne (Phiz).

73 (above) Attributed to J. & W. Ridgway

The Fountain, Trinity College, Cambridge (A)
Moulded and pierced fruit basket (c 1814-20), in dark blue, with a view of the Great Court of Trinity College, Cambridge inside. The border has trumpet-shaped flowers and scrolled medallions with two themes—children feeding a goat and children milking a goat. This occupies the space between the piercing and the indented rim both inside and outside the basket. The moulded handles are covered with a very deep blue translucent glaze.
Unmarked.
Length 24.9cm (9.8in). Width 14cm (5.5in). Height from base to top of handles 11.2cm (4in). Slightly rippled pale blue glaze.

74 (below) Attributed to J. & W. Ridgway

The Fountain, Trinity College, Cambridge (A)
A similar moulded and pierced basket (c 1814-20) differing from 73 (above) only in the moulding of the sides and the handles which rise more sharply from the edge.
Length 23.4cm (9.2in). Width 13.4cm (5.3in). Height from base to top of handles 11.4 cm (4.5in).

Some of the engravings in the Ridgway series have been adapted from the original Phiz drawings in *The Old Curiosity Shop;* that of Little Nell and her grandfather looking back towards St Paul's Cathedral for example, but most have been designed specially. The feeding bottle (75) is printed in blue with a scene showing Little Nell walking beside a river with the figures of two women in the distance. It illustrates a passage from Chapter XLII:

'In one of these wanderings in the evening time, when following the two sisters at a humble distance, she felt, in her sympathy with them and her recognition of their trials of something akin to her own loneliness of spirit, a comfort and consolation which made such moments a time of deep delight'.

Many firms made feeding bottles printed with blue patterns but few are marked. Among marked examples are those of Copeland & Garrett and Wedgwood (Coysh, plate 138).

Ridgway, Morley, Wear & Co

In 1836, William Ridgway's daughter married Francis Morley and a company was formed by Ridgway, Morley and a third party called Wear. This company took over the pottery of Hicks, Meigh & Johnson at Shelton. The plate (76) is of particular interest since it bears the pattern name EGLINTOUN and was clearly made soon after 1839 to commemorate the famous Eglinton Tournament of that year staged by Lord Eglinton in his Castle grounds in Ayrshire. The event, for which all the participants wore medieval costume, was unfortunately something of an anticlimax for it poured with rain all day. (See Anstruther, I. *The Knight and the Umbrella.* 1963). It is interesting to note that W. Ridgway, Son & Co also 'published' an Elginton moulded jug on 1 September, 1840.

John & Richard Riley of Burslem

The dish (77) is illustrated as an example of Riley's work and as a variation of the 'Scene after Claude Lorraine' also produced by Leeds Old Pottery (Coysh, plate 55). The Riley version has two bridges and two classical ladies are seen below the central tree whereas the Leeds version has a fisherman.

75 (above left) Attributed to William Ridgway, Son & Co   'Humphrey's Clock' Series
'Little Nell by the river' (A)
(Courtesy: Robin Gurnett, Esq)
Infant feeding bottle (1838-46) in medium blue, with a view of Little Nell walking near a river bank in the countryside. A 'border' of scrolls and diamond-shaped motifs decorates the edge of the bottle.
Unmarked.
Length 17.3cm (6.7in). Smooth clear glaze on white moulded body.

76 (above right) Ridgway, Morley, Wear & Co
Eglinton Pattern (A)
(Courtesy: Mr and Mrs Martin Pulver)
Indented plate (c 1839-42), in light-medium blue, with a central group of tournament accoutrements including armour, a shield, lance, sword and flags. The border pattern is made up of tiny fleur-de-lys motifs within a beaded edge. The inner edge has dagger-style stringing.
Printed mark: R. M. W. & CO. beneath a group of tournament accoutrements across which a ribbon hangs with the word EGLINTOUN (an earlier spelling of the name 'Eglinton')
Diam 26.8cm (10.5in). Double foot rim, the inner part rounded. Smooth pale blue glaze.

77 (below) John and Richard Riley
'Scene after Claude Lorraine'
Indented dish (c 1814-28), in medium blue, with a scene showing a classical building on a rocky promontory above a river which is crossed by two bridges, the nearer bridge with three arches, the distant bridge with eight arches. There are boatmen on the river bank. A monopteros and a waterfall are prominent features. The border consists of a panorama of country scenes separated from the central scene by acanthus stringing.
Printed mark: RILEY on a ribbon superimposed on a flower.
Impressed mark: 20
Length 53.1cm (20.9in). Width 39.6cm (15.6in). No foot rim. Colourless rippled glaze.

John Rogers & Son of Longport

John Rogers and Son produced a very large number of designs for the home market but limited their American patterns, so far as we know, to two— *The Boston State House* (Coysh, plate 94) and *The City Hall, New York*. Most other potters exporting to America produced a larger number of special patterns for that market. Some indication of the proportions made for both markets or for America alone can be gained from the check lists given by Moore and Laidekker. Enoch Wood used 315 different patterns of which 87 were special American views; J. & R. Clews 163, including 53 American views; Ralph Hall 114, mainly of English views; Adams 109, including 20 American views; and J. & W. Ridgway 55 of which 40 were American views. In all about 40 Staffordshire firms are known to have been exporting to America in the 1815-50 period and between them they used over 1,200 different patterns. There were many other potters who did not mark their wares.

These figures emphasize the fact that a good collection can be made of patterns from a single factory, especially of the wares of firms which catered mainly for the home market—Davenport, Rogers, Spode and Wedgwood. Twelve such patterns by Rogers have already been illustrated (Coysh, plates 79-93). Four more are illustrated here (78-81).

The earlier illustrations led to the identification of the sources of certain Rogers' patterns. A print collector discovered the *Camel Pattern* (Coysh, plate 84) to be the 'Gate leading to Musjed at Chanar Ghun' and it has since been discovered that the *Monopteros Pattern* (Coysh, plates 86-7) shows the 'Remains of an Ancient Building near Firoz Shah's Cotilla, Delhi'. These scenes are derived from T. and W. Daniell's *Oriental Scenery and Views in Hindoostan* published by Robert Bowyer of the Historic Gallery, Pall Mall, between 1795 and 1807. The title of this Rogers' series should therefore be changed to the *Oriental Scenery Series*.

It may be worth expressing some doubt once more about a maritime series with a shell and seaweed border and views of sailing vessels such as the Shannon and Chesapeake. This is invariably attributed to Rogers but is there any real evidence that it was produced by this pottery? The author has examined many examples, all unmarked, and can still trace no record of a marked piece.

The attribution of a topographical series which bears a cartouche with named views is discussed later (pp 102).

78 (above left) *John Rogers & Son*
                                        Greek Statue Pattern (A)
(*Courtesy: Mrs V. Heap*)
Slightly indented plate (1814-36), in dark medium blue, with a scene of classical ruins. A waterfall descends over a rocky outcrop on the left and there is a statue on a plinth surrounded by broken masonry on the right. Two figures rest by the masonry. The border is of scrolled acanthus leaves and a scallop motif.
Impressed mark: ROGERS
Diam 24.9cm (9.8in). Single foot rim. Greenish blue rippled glaze.

79 (above right) *John Rogers & Son*
                                        The Fruit and Flowers Pattern (A)
(*Courtesy: Mrs V. Heap*)
Indented plate (1814-36), in medium blue, with a design of fruit and flowers. Behind these is a vase or urn decorated with a standing Chinese figure. The border consists of two bands, the inner of stylised flowers and leaves; the rim has a catherine-wheel motif.
Impressed mark: ROGERS
Diam 20.8cm (8.2in). Single foot rim. Rippled blue glaze.

80 (below left) *John Rogers & Son*
                                        'Florence' Pattern
(*Courtesy: Mrs V. Heap*)
Indented dished plate (c 1825-36), in medium and dark blue, with an Italian scene with a river, a three-arch bridge, riverside buildings, and a gondola with a gondolier. On the left a figure is seated on steps below a large flower-filled urn. The border is of scrolled floral panels broken by four identical panels with an Italian river with buildings and boats.
Impressed mark: ROGERS
Printed mark: FLORENCE *in a floral cartouche*
Diam 26.2cm (10.3in). Rounded foot rim. Smooth pale blue glaze.

81 (below right) *John Rogers & Son*
                                        'Pompeii' Pattern
(*Courtesy: Mrs V. Heap*)
Dished plate (c 1825-36) with a shaped indented edge, in light and medium blue, with an egret surrounded by acanthus-type scrolled foliage. The border has several motifs alternately in light and dark blue. Swags with birds, sea serpents or masks are in light blue. These alternate with groups of military accoutrements or reclining ladies beside urns.
Impressed mark: ROGERS *and 8*
Diam 25.7cm (10.1in). Rounded foot rim. Blue glaze.

William Smith & Co of Stockton-on-Tees

William Smith operated the Stafford Pottery on the south side of the River Tees at Stockton from 1825 to 1855. He was an enterprising potter who brought Mr John Whalley from Staffordshire to manage the works and introduced machinery and 'modern' methods. The tea bowl and saucer (82) is of fine quality. This *Tea Party Pattern* originated from an engraving by Robert Hancock for a black print on Battersea enamel (see Turner, W. *Transfer Printing on Enamels, Porcelain and Pottery.* 1907. plate A4). Another version, also by Hancock, was used for a red print on Bow porcelain (*ibid.* plate A6). It appears later with slight variations in black on Liverpool and Wedgwood wares (*ibid.* plates A8 and A21) and also on Cockpit Heath Derby wares where the dog appears for the first time (*ibid.* plate 18). Early in the nineteenth century the pattern was used by Sewell of St. Anthony Pottery, Newcastle-upon-Tyne printed in red overglaze.

The use of blue-printing with colour printing is very rare indeed. The Smith plate (83) has a wide border in underglaze blue and a central pattern in the well of the plate of a basket of fruit in three colours—green, yellow and red. Although William Smith & Co are known to have used colour printing fairly soon after its introduction by F. & R. Pratt & Co (see Ball, A. *Price Guide to Pot Lids.* p 464), no previous example has been recorded in association with a blue-printed border.

Since this plate is impressed with the mark WEDGEWOOD which William Smith & Co were restrained from using after 1848 (see p 96) there can be little doubt that it was produced between 1845 and 1848 prior to the Great Exhibition when colour printing started to gain in popularity.

Spode of Stoke-on-Trent

The Spode collector has depended for many years on the valuable book by S. B. Williams on *Antique Blue and White Spode*, first published in 1943. Since then little was written on the subject until Leonard Whiter's book on *Spode* (1970) which gives the collector many of the original names used by the factory to describe blue and white patterns. Many patterns have been known for years by other names; to prevent confusion the factory name is given in the captions and reference to other names in the text.

Spode's *Queen Charlotte Pattern* (84) is the name used by the factory for a chinoiserie scene because

82 (above left) William Smith & Co
'Tea Party' Pattern
Tea bowl and saucer (c 1825-30), in dark blue, with a scene showing a lady and gentleman taking tea. A servant stands close by filling a teapot from a kettle. A small dog sits up and begs. The tea bowl carries this scene in a medallion on one side, and a country scene with a shepherd and sheep in a medallion on the other side. The border on the saucer and inside the bowl is of star-shaped flowers with leaves on a stipple ground.
Printed mark on saucer: W. SMITH & CO. in a scrolled cartouche.
Diam of bowl 8.3cm (3.3in) and of saucer 13.5cm (5.3in). Both have foot rims. Greenish-blue glaze.

83 (above right) William Smith & Co
'Fruit Basket' Pattern
Dished plate (c 1845) with many indentations, printed with a wide light blue border which extends into the well and is made up of alternate oblique stripes with flower sprays, a marbled motif and fruit sprays. The central design with the fruit basket is colour-printed in green, yellow and red.
Impressed mark: W. S. & CO's with '42'
WEDGEWOOD
Printed mark: FRUIT BASKET printed on a basket of fruit beneath which is the maker's mark W. S. & CO.
Diam 26cm (10.2in). Rounded foot rim. Smooth blue glaze.

84 (below) Spode Spode's 'Queen Charlotte' Pattern
Dish (c 1815-20), in medium dark blue, with a Chinese scene with pagodas and a single-arch bridge. Two figures on the bridge face the main pagoda in front of which a pathway leads to two trees behind which figures appear to be hiding. The border has cellular motifs, scrolls and dark blue striped lozenges.
Impressed mark: SPODE (Whiter 4) with the number 1
Printed mark: SPODE (Whiter 16a)
Length 52cm (20.5in). Width 41.2cm (16.2in). A foot rim 2.5cm high raises one end of the dish so that meat juices may drain down shallow channels to a a gravy well at the other end. Smooth blue glaze.

it is thought that Queen Charlotte may have bought wares with this design when she visited the Spode works in 1817. This is in some ways unfortunate since the Worcester Porcelain Factory produced a different Queen Charlotte pattern with alternating spirals of underglaze blue and on-glaze reds and golds. It is therefore important to refer to the Spode pattern as *Spode's Queen Charlotte Pattern*. Whiter (p 150) states that the only examples he has seen have been on china. However, the large dish (84) makes it clear that it was used on earthenwares. The pattern has also been noted on a fine pair of unmarked earthenware candlesticks and on a bordaloue in the Wellcome Institute Collection, also unmarked. The border on these earthenware examples differs from that on the china plate illustrated by Whiter (plate 17) which includes an insect.

The interest of *Spode's Queen Charlotte Pattern* is in the long pathway that leads to a pair of trees behind which two figures appear to be hiding, perhaps from pursuers crossing the bridge.

Spode's *Indian Sporting Series* is well known (Coysh, pp 72-5). The lidded toilet dish (85) makes an interesting use of part of the border from this series, using only the bear and the bird. The use to which this dish was put is in some doubt. It was probably for toothsticks. Already in Georgian times, considerable trouble was taken to keep the teeth clean. Toothsticks and powders were advertised and many 'home recipes' were in use including 'lemon juice, mixed with burnt alum and salt, rubbed on a clean rag wrapped around the end of a stick'. (See Burton E. *The Georgians at Home*. 1967, p. 335)

The cover of a similar dish (86) has ventilation holes. This lid has a very rare pattern—*The Village Scene*. Only one other example has so far been recorded—a covered toilet pot (Whiter plate 64). On this pot the villagers are seen around a decorated pole, though not a typical maypole. The rest of the pattern is on the cover which is seen to better advantage here (86). In the case of both pieces the border consists of a continuous band of white scrolls on a blue ground.

The bordaloue (87) carries another rather uncommon design—*The Old Peacock Pattern*. Whiter states that this is a late Spode production. This particular example is from the Wellcome Institute Collection which is described fully by J. K. Crellin in *Medical Ceramics in the Wellcome Institute* Vol 1. 1969.

85 (above) Spode   *'Indian Sporting Series' Border Pattern*
(*Courtesy: Mr and Mrs Martin Pulver*)
Earthenware toilet dish and cover (c 1810), in medium blue, with an Indian scene with bear and bird. The border has an acanthus-leaf-style motif on a stipple ground. The scene is printed on the cover, on the inside of the dish and (on a smaller scale) around the vertical sides of the dish. The border is also printed inside the vertical sides of the dish.
Impressed mark: SPODE (*Whiter 4*)
               49
Length 18.8cm (7in). Width 6.3cm (2.5in)
Printed mark: SPODE *and a large 'A' (Whiter 16a)*

86 (centre) Spode   *'Village Scene' Pattern*
(*Courtesy: Mr and Mrs Martin Pulver*)
Earthenware toilet dish cover (c 1810-20) in medium blue, with a scene in which a man and woman dance to the music provided by a second man playing a serpent. The border is of white scrolls on a dark ground.
Printed mark: SPODE (*Whiter 16a*)
Length 19.5cm (7.6in). Width 7.1cm (2.8in). The lid contains three pierced holes, slightly out of alignment. Smooth blue glaze.

87 (below) Spode   *'Old Peacock' Pattern*
(*Courtesy: The Wellcome Trustees*)
Bourdaloue (c 1825-33), printed in medium blue, with a design of flowers, and peacocks amid foliage.
Printed mark: SPODE (*Whiter 16a*)
Length 24cm (9.5in). No foot rim.

A bordaloue was a personal pot used originally by the ladies of Versailles in the reign of Louis XIV. These 'female urinals', as they are called in the Institute Catalogue, were named after a priest, Louis Bordaloue (1632-1704) who preached such long Lenten sermons at the French Court in 1675 that the ladies found it necessary to conceal a china receptacle in the pew beneath their skirts. These receptacles were made of Chinese porcelain and continued to be used long after the death of Bordaloue. An example decorated in famille rose enamels and bearing the coat of arms of Madame la Pompadour (1721-64) was illustrated in *The Collectors' Guide* for August, 1969, page 7.

Blue-printed bordaloues were made in the 1830-60 period. Marked examples have been noted made by Davenport, Spode and Wedgwood. It is certain that other potters produced them (143). Even in the 1860s they were still being produced by Cork, Edge and Malkin of Burslem.

Spode's *Caramanian Series* based on engravings in Luigi Mayer's *Views in Egypt, Palestine and the Ottoman Empire* (1801-4) are greatly sought after by collectors. Some examples have already been illustrated (Coysh, plates 101-2). Those illustrated here (88-93) have all been acquired recently by collectors: indeed, part-dinner services still crop up from time to time in auction sales.

The engravers of these views often adapted several different illustrations from Mayer's book for one pattern so that many of the patterns are composite pictures. In the *City of Corinth* (88) the ancient temple has been superimposed on the original view and the boat has also been taken from another illustration.

The rectangular dish (90) with a view of the *Citadel near Corinth* has been reversed. Examples are known both with the bridge on the left and the bridge on the right (Williams, Fig 51). There is apparently no engraving in Luigi Mayer's book which corresponds to this Spode pattern though it does describe a citadel 'called Acrocorinthus, built on a steep rock overlooking the city, which was almost impregnable.'

The gravy tureen (91) and plate (92) with the view of the *Ancient Granary at Cacamo* show how a view is adapted to suit the shape of the piece on which it is printed. The central archway remains roughly the same as do the three figures within it and the three figures to the left. The design on the plate, however, includes a large building with pediment and sculptured frieze from another engraving and the tureen includes three additional

*88 (above left) Spode   'Caramanian Series'
                                'City of Corinth'*
Dished indented plate (c 1810), in medium blue, with two horsemen travelling away from a city and a man walking ahead with a dog. The border of Indian scenes is separated from the central picture by a narrow band of S-scrolls.
Impressed mark: SPODE (Whiter 3) and 2
Diam 25.5cm (10in). No foot rim. Pale greenish-blue rippled glaze.

*89 (above right) Spode   'Carmanian Series'
            'Necropolis' or 'Cemetery at Cacamo'*
(Courtesy: Robin Gurnett, Esq)
Indented plate (c 1810), in medium blue, with a view of the Necropolis or Cemetery at Cacamo. The sarcophagi are in the middle distance beyond a stretch of water on which there are several boats. The border of Indian scenes is separated from the central picture by a narrow band of S-scrolls.
Impressed mark: SPODE (Whiter 3)
Diam 21.5cm (8.4in). No foot rim. Pale greenish-blue rippled glaze.

*90 (below) Spode   'Caramanian Series'
                            'Citadel near Corinth'*
(Courtesy: Robin Gurnett, Esq)
Rectangular dish with rounded corners (c 1810), in medium blue, with a view of the citadel near Corinth showing a bridge with three figures, one carrying a pack. A ruin with pillars stands on a hill beyond the river and there is a domed building in the distance. Three boatmen approach two men working on the river bank. The border of Indian scenes is separated from the central picture by a narrow band of S-scrolls.
Impressed mark: SPODE (Whiter 3)
Length 27.1cm (11.6in). Width 19.7cm (7.2in).
Flattened foot rim. Greenish-blue rippled glaze.

figures from *An Ancient Bath at Cacamo in Cara-mania* (93). This is the first time that this pattern of the Ancient Bath has been recorded in the Spode Caramanian series and it must be added to the patterns already known. The list to date is now:

The Castle of Boudron (Williams, Fig 41)
An Ancient Bath at Cacamo (93)
Ancient Granary at Cacamo (91-2)
Necropolis or Cemetery at Cacamo (89)
Sarcophagi at Cacamo (Williams, Fig 61)
Obelisk at Catania
Sarcophagi and Sepulchres at the Head of the
    Harbour at Cacamo (Coysh, plate 102)
The Harbour Entrance at Cacamo (Williams,
    Fig 45)
City of Corinth (88)
Citadel near Corinth (90)
Antique Fragments at Limosso (Williams,
    Fig 43)
The Harbour at Macri (Williams, Fig 66)
Colossal Sarcophagus near Castle Rosso
    (Williams, Fig 65)
Triumphal Arch at Tripoli in Barbary (Coysh,
    plate 101)

A number of unmarked examples of the *Colossal Sarcophagus near Castle Rosso* have been noted which appear to have been made by another potter.

The *Temple-Landscape, Second* (94) was apparently used only on stone china or new stone. Both marks occur with this pattern. It was probably introduced c 1820.

91 (above left) Spode   'Caramanian Series'
               'Ancient Granary at Cacamo'
Gravy tureen (c 1810), in medium blue, with a view of an archway among ruins. The figures to the left are as in 92. To the right are three larger figures, taken from 'An Ancient Bath at Cacamo' (93) *one with a staff. The border inside the tureen is from the same source as Indian Sporting Series with wild boar, cattle, and a groom with a horse. The handles of the tureen, in the shape of the heads of animals with mouths wide open, are covered printed with shamrock leaves and flowers.*
Impressed mark: Spode (*Whiter 3*) *and 3*
Length 18.5cm (7.3in). Flattened foot rim. Greenish-blue glaze.

92 (above right) Spode   'Caramanian Series'
               'Ancient Granary at Cacamo'
Indented plate (c 1810), in medium blue, with a view of a ruined archway to the right of a granary with sculptured frieze and pediment. Six figures are to be seen—three in the archway and three in the courtyard before the granary. The border of Indian scenes is separated from the central picture by a narrow band of S-scrolls.
Impressed mark: Spode (*Whiter 3*) *and 13.*
Diam 16.3cm (6.4in). No foot rim. Pale greenish-blue rippled glaze.

93 (below left) Spode   'Caramanian Series'
         'An Ancient Bath at Cacamo in Caramania'
(Courtesy: Robin Gurnett, Esq)
Indented plate (c 1810), in medium blue, with a scene of a triple archway with steps on which figures come and go. The border of Indian scenes is separated from the central picture by a narrow band of S-scrolls.
Impressed mark: Spode (*Whiter 3*) *and 7*
Diam 19cm (7.4in). No foot rim. Pale greenish-blue rippled glaze.

94 (below right) Spode 'Temple Landscape' Second'
(Courtesy: Robin Gurnett, Esq)
Indented dished plate (c 1820), in medium-dark blue, with a scene with pagodas and a bridge in the foreground on which there is a man carrying an open parasol. The scene is framed in a continuous blue band. The border is a variant of the 'Temple border' (Whiter p 136) with insects and geometrical motifs. Between the scene and the border is a cellular band 1.3cm (0.5in) wide.
Impressed mark: SPODES
             NEW STONE (*Whiter Mark 7*)
Diam 24cm (9.4in). Double unglazed foot rim. Thick bluish white glaze retracted near foot rim. Heavy body. Weight nearly 1 lb 6 oz.

Spode: Miscellaneous Patterns

Spode collectors have, from time to time, given names to particular patterns which did not conform to those used by the Spode factory. Leonard Whiter in his book on *Spode* (1970) has, when possible, made the factory names available and these should clearly be used in all future references. The designs originally referred to by S. B. Williams as *The Hundred Antiques Patterns* should now be called the *Trophies Patterns* of which there were three types:

1. *The Nankin Border and Trophy Centre (Trophies-Nankin)*
2. *The Etruscan Border and Trophy Centre (Trophies-Etruscan)*
3. *The Dagger Border and Trophy Centre (Trophies-Dagger)*

The first was illustrated by the author (Coysh, plate 15) as *The Hundred Antiques Pattern—First version*. The second was illustrated by S. B. Williams simply as *The Hundred Antiques Pattern*. It is here included under its correct title (95). All three are illustrated together by Whiter (plates 28-30).

The design named the *Bamboo and Rock Pattern* (96) appears to be rare on earthenware and this example is unusual since the bamboo has been enamelled overglaze in yellow. Whiter illustrates an example of this pattern (plate 157) in the centre of a porcelain dish and refers to it as 'Pattern 1185, red and gold.' This example bears the rare Prince of Wales mark and for this reason Whiter dates the introduction of this pattern to c 1806. It was almost certainly used on earthenware at a later date since the impressed mark (Whiter 4a) has clear serifs on the capital 'S' which would suggest a date some ten years later i.e. c 1816.

The Fence Pattern (97) is considered to be an early production, a version of which was described by Williams as the *Chinese Floral Pattern*. This carries the border of the *Group Pattern* (99).

The design named *British Flowers II* (98) has the same border as a pattern with this name illustrated by Whiter (Plate 52). The central designs on these plates clearly correspond roughly to those on plates with the *Botanical Patterns* (Coysh, plates 119 and 120).

The *Group Pattern* (99) is early. Whiter states that 'the first enamelled version of this pattern was Number 1437, c 1809'.

The Milkmaid Pattern (100) carries the same border as the Tower Pattern (Coysh, plate 107) and seems to have been used mainly on tewares.

95 (above left) Spode 'Trophies—Etruscan' Pattern Indented plate (c 1825-33), in medium blue, with a design based on the 'Trophies-Nankin' pattern. Etruscan border motifs and flower sprays decorate the trophies.
Impressed mark: SPODE (Whiter 4) and 27
Printed mark: SPODE (Whiter 16a)
Diam 24.9cm (9.8in). No foot rim. Slightly rippled blue glaze.

96 (above right) Spode 'Bamboo and Rock' Pattern (A) Plate (c 1816), printed in medium blue, with the bamboo enamelled overglaze in yellow.
Impressed mark: SPODE (Whiter 4)
Printed mark: SPODE (Whiter 16a)
Diam 20.2cm (8in). Recessed base forming prominent foot rim. Slightly rippled pale blue glaze.

97 (centre left) Spode 'Fence' Pattern (Courtesy: Robin Gurnett, Esq) Plate (c 1810), in medium blue, with chinoiserie including bamboo, willow and flowers. The bamboo and willow areas are separated by a fence. The border around the edge of the rim is of hexagonal cells.
Impressed mark: SPODE (Whiter 2a)
Diam 18.5cm (7.3in). No foot rim. Slightly rippled greenish-blue glaze on cream-coloured body.

98 (centre right) Spode British Flowers II (A) Indented plate (c 1828-33), in medium blue, with a spray of flowers. The border is of leaf scrolls and flowers.
Impressed mark: SPODE (Whiter 4) and 54
Printed mark: SPODE (Whiter 16a)
Diam 15cm (9.8in). Colourless slightly rippled glaze.

99 (below left) Spode 'Group' Pattern Dish (c 1810-20) with cusped edge, in medium blue, with central floral group with a butterfly. This is enclosed in a cellular band with geometrical motifs. Four groups of flowers decorate the rounded corners and the whole is enclosed in a band of geometrical motifs.
Impressed mark: SPODE (Whiter 4) and 24
Printed mark: SPODE (Whiter 16a). Recessed base.
Greenish blue rippled glaze.

100 (below right) Spode 'Milkmaid' Pattern (Courtesy: Robin Gurnett, Esq) Teapot (c 1814-20), in medium blue, with a scene of a woman kneeling and milking a cow. Two calves rest nearby. The border of flowers and dark blue leaves against a stipple ground, is repeated on spout and handle. The lid carries part of the milkmaid scene.
Printed mark: SPODE (Whiter 16a)
Height 6.3cm (2.5in). Foot rim slightly splayed and rounded. Smooth pale blue glaze.

Spode's *Marble Pattern* (101) has carried a number of different names including *Mosaic* and *Cracked Ice and Prunus*. It was introduced c 1821 and was without doubt derived from the pattern found on imported ginger jars. The cracked ice is meant to represent the end of winter and the prunus blossom the coming of spring.

The examples shown are in earthenware but this pattern is often found on 'Spode's New Stone' and was continued into the Copeland & Garrett period.

The shapes can be identified from the Spode 1920 Shape Book (see Whiter, Chapter 7). The cup has the 'London' shape which was introduced c 1813 and had become the most popular Spode shape by 1820. It is still in use today. The jug has the 'Antique' shape.

The *Lattice Scroll Pattern* (102) was a popular design introduced c 1810. It was used for special services (Whiter, plate 79) and as a border on large pieces such as garden seats (Whiter, plate 100).

101 (above) Spode   *'Marble' Pattern*
(Jug by Courtesy: Mrs P. Trethowan)
Saucer (c 1821-33), in medium-dark blue, with a pattern of stylised flowers in white against a line-engraved mosaic ground.
Impressed mark: 3
Printed mark: SPODE (Whiter 16a)
Diam 14.3cm (5.6in). Inside of saucer without ridge. Rounded foot rim. Smooth blue glaze.
Cup (c 1821-33) of 'London' shape in medium-dark blue, with overall marble pattern outside and a border of mosaic pattern inside with a central medallion in the base.
Printed mark: SPODE (Whiter 16a)
Diam 9.3cm (3.1in). Foot rim splayed and rounded. Blue glaze.
Jug (c 1821-33) of 'Antique' shape in medium-dark blue, with marble pattern.
Printed mark: SPODE (Whiter 16a)
Height to top of handle 14.2cm (5.6in). Colourless glaze.

102 (below) Spode   *'Lattice Scroll' Pattern*
Dish (c 1810-33), in medium blue, with a central pattern of flowers and leaves. The wide border has stylised leaves and flowers linked by lattice-work and scrolls.
Impressed mark: SPODE (Whiter 2a)
     42
Printed mark: SPODE (Whiter 16a) with a small triangle.
Length 26.9cm (10.6in). Width 19.6cm (7.7in). Foot rim follows the outline shape of the rim and raises the dish 8mm (0.3in). Smooth blue glaze.

Spode's Aesop's Fables Series

Spode's *Aesop's Fables Series* was a late introduction between c 1830 and 1833, and wares were
later made in the Copeland & Garrett period with
these patterns printed in green. By the time the
series came on the market makers were beginning
to mark their wares not only with their own mark
but also with the name of the pattern, usually in the
form of a cartouche. Minton marks of the period,
for example, usually carried a pattern name. The
Aesop's Fables series was printed with the title of
the fable and in the case of the ewer (103) with two
titles; one for the scene on each side. Were these
patterns specially designed or were they based on
one of the many editions of Aesop's Fables? Here
is another field for research.

A collection of the complete list of fables used
by Spode and Copeland & Garrett would be worth-
while acquisition. It should not be too difficult since
individual dinner services used many fables as
illustrations. (See Whiter, plates 89 and 90). A
tentative and no doubt incomplete list is given:

> The Dog in the Manger
> The Dog and the Shadow (103)
> The Dog and the Sheep
> The Fox and the Lion
> The Hare and the Tortoise
> The Mountain in Labour (103)
> The Wolf and the Crane
> The Wolf, the Lamb and the Goat
> The Sow and the Wolf.

103 Spode   'Aesop's Fables' Series
(Courtesy: Mr and Mrs Martin Pulver)
*Moulded ewer (c 1830-33), in medium blue, with
scenes from Aesop's Fables. On one side is a scene
illustrating 'The Dog and the Shadow' fable; on the
other side is a scene depicting 'The Mountains in
Labour' fable. The base and rim border patterns are
of flowers and scrolls. One scroll ends with the head
of a fox. The border is repeated inside the ewer.
Beneath the spout and handle are floral sprays. The
handle has a stipple ground.*
*Printed marks show the names of the patterns—on one
side* THE DOG AND THE SHADOW *and on
the other side* THE MOUNTAINS IN LABOUR.
These appear on a wide scroll with the series title
AESOP'S FABLES *beneath and the name* SPODE.
The scroll has a background of floral sprays.
*Height of ewer to top of handle 27.3cm (10.7in). Diam
of base 12.4cm (4.8in). Height to top of handle
25.1cm (9.9in). Flattened foot rim. Smooth colourless
glaze on white body.*

Wares marked 'Stevenson'

An impressed mark of a three-masted ship with the surname Stevenson above it, the whole sometimes enclosed within an ellipse, occurs on blue-printed wares bearing various patterns: The Chinese Traders Pattern (104) and the Birds and Willow Pattern (105) are examples. At various times this mark has been attributed to Andrew Stevenson (GM3700), Ralph Stevenson of Cobridge (Rhead, G. W. British Pottery Marks, 1910, p 253) and James Stevenson of Greenock Pottery (Fleming, J. A. Scottish Pottery. Glasgow, 1923). T. H. Ormsbee in English China and Its Marks (New York, 1959. London, 1962) attributed the mark within the ellipse to Andrew Stevenson and the mark with no ellipse to Ralph Stevenson.

The facts about these potters are as follows:
1. Andrew Stevenson of Cobridge started his pottery c 1808 in partnership with Bucknall who retired c 1816. Andrew Stevenson continued the business and built up an American trade. The mark used on these pieces was A. STEVENSON STAFFORDSHIRE WARRANTED between concentric circles surrounding a crown (a variant of GM3701). This mark was also used on English scenes printed in dark blue (Coysh, plate 124). L. Jewitt in The Ceramic Art of Great Britain (1883) states that Stevenson's Cobridge works were closed in 1819 and passed into the hands of James Clews. G. A. Godden, on the other hand, states that James and Ralph Clews rented the Cobridge Works from William Adams. It appears that confusion has arisen over the use of the term 'Cobridge Works' instead of 'works at Cobridge'. The dates given by Godden for the period when Andrew Stevenson was operating at Cobridge (i.e. 1818-30) are no doubt correct since his American export trade was mainly after 1818.
2. Ralph Stevenson operated the Lower Manufactory at Cobridge c 1810-32 when he formed a partnership with his sons until 1835. There was a short period, however, c 1825, when he was in partnership with A. L. Williams. Printed marks include R. STEVENSON, or R. S. and later R. STEVENSON & SON, or R. S. & S. For a short period c 1825 the mark was STEVENSON & WILLIAMS printed in a cartouche or R. S. W. Ralph Stevenson also had an important American trade and on these export wares, which were printed in dark blue, he used either a vine leaf or an oak and acorn border.
3. James Stevenson was appointed by James and

104 (above left) Stevenson
                    The Chinese Traders Pattern (A)
(Courtesy: Robin Gurnett, Esq)
Dished indented plate (c 1816-30), in medium blue, with a Chinese scene with traders carrying produce across a waterway. Other figures watch them from an open verandah-type building. The border is of figures (one with a stringed instrument), lake scenes and trees separated by C-scrolls and geometrical motifs. The engraving is signed—'Wear Sc.'
Impressed mark: Stevenson above three-masted ship (variant of GM 3700 and 3700 but without the enclosing ellipse)
Diam 25cm (9.9in). No foot rim. Clear rippled glaze on white body.

105 (above right) Stevenson
                    Ornithological Series (A)
                    Birds and Willow Pattern (A)
Indented plate (c 1815-30), in medium blue, with a scene with birds at rest and in flight against a background of trees (which include a willow) and shrubs. The scene is framed in a band of small leaves and flowers. The border pattern consists of sprays of flowers in scrolled panels against a background mosaic of small catherine wheels.
Impressed mark: Stevenson above a three-masted ship (GM 1814 and 3700 but without the enclosing ellipse.)

106 (below left) Attributed to Stevenson
                    Ornithological Series (A)
                    The Peacock Pattern (A)
Indented plate (c 1816-30) in medium blue, with a scene of trees, flowers and birds in which a peacock is prominent. Border as in 105.
Unmarked.
Diam 25.1cm (9.9in). Rippled blue glaze.

107 (below right) Attributed to Stevenson
                    Ornithological Series (A)
                    Pheasant Pattern (A)
Deep eight-sided dish (c 1815-30), in medium blue, each side with serpentine curve. The central scene shows birds at rest and in flight, including a pheasant perched on a branch. Border as in 105 above.
Unmarked.
Length 36.8cm (14.5in). Width 28.7cm (11.3in). Deep foot rim 0.8cm (.35in). Rippled blue glaze.

Andrew Muir to be the manager of their Clyde Pottery at Greencok which started to produce in 1816. The *Glasgow Courier* of 5 November 1816, in a notice to shippers, stated that the Clyde Pottery Company was making 'printed earthenware of a quality which they can with confidence recommend'. The author is informed by the Greenock Museum that it owns a blue-printed bowl which combines a three-masted ship with the mark CLYDE POTTERY, GREENOCK.

About 1820 James Stevenson set up on his own in the Greenock Pottery. J. Arnold Fleming states that James Stevenson & Co 'stamped their wares with the mark of a ship inside a narrow oval garter'. Later Stevenson sold the pottery to Thomas Shirley & Co to concentrate on the retail business in which he had always been involved. He certainly had a retail connection as early as 1810 for in that year when Josiah Wedgwood II asked his chief traveller, Josiah Bateman, to collect information about the wares of other makers, Bateman replied that he had seen some Spode plates 'at Messrs. Stevenson's at Glasgow'. It could well be that the three-masted ship was, in fact, Stevenson's retail mark. It would be an appropriate symbol for Fleming tells us that 'Greenock was an important market for the New-foundland seal-fishers who carried back large quantities of pottery among other merchandise in payment for their oil'.

To all these facts about the three potters to whom the ship mark has been attributed must be added a statement by Jewitt. 'There was more than one firm of potters with this name (Stevenson) in Staffordshire. Some were at Cobridge. One used a vesica-shaped mark bearing a three-masted ship with the name Stevenson above it impressed in the ware'. He does not, however, state which particular Stevenson used this mark.

One more clue is available. The print of the *Chinese Traders Pattern* (104) is signed 'Wear Sc.'. This would appear to the Wear of the Staffordshire engraving firm of Bentley, Wear & Bourne inscribed on a plate by C. J. Mason & Co. (Little, plate 39).

However, attribution of the Stevenson ship mark must remain in doubt until some further evidence is available.

Swansea: The Cambrian Pottery

Early examples of blue-printed wares made at the Cambrian Pottery in Swansea are in the Chinese taste. A number are described in a valuable paper by W. J. Grant Davidson on *Early Swansea Pottery*,

Note: View page 85 from outer edge.
108 (above left) Attributed to Stevenson
Ornithological Series (A)
The Kingfisher Pattern (A)
Indented dish (c 1816-30), in medium blue, with a scene with trees, flowers and birds of which a king-fisher is the species most readily recognised. Border as in 105.
Unmarked.
Length 38.1cm (15in). Width 32.3cm (12.7in). No foot rim. Rippled blue glaze.

109 (above right) Attributed to Stevenson
Ornothological Series (A)
Birds of Prey Pattern (A)
Indented dish (c 1816-30), in medium blue, with a scene of trees, flowers and birds in which two vultures are the most prominent. Border as in 105.
Unmarked.
Length 48.5cm (19.1in). Width 37.1cm (14.6in). No foot rim. Rippled blue glaze.

110 (below left) Attributed to Cambrian Pottery, Swansea   *'Chinese Scene after Pillement'*
Dish (c 1800) with a scene with four Chinese figures, one holding a parasol, against a background of decorative fences and vases of flowers. A bird struts in the foreground. The picture is framed in a scalloped printed band of geometrical motifs and a similar band extends from the edge of the dish towards the centre.
Unmarked.
Diam 18.7cm (7.3in). The foot rim is not reflected inside the dish where there is a smooth curved surface. Greenish-blue glaze.

111 (below right) Cambrian Pottery, Swansea
'Elephant Pattern'
Indented plate (c 1800), in dark-medium blue, a fence, and a background of peony flowers and a willow tree. The stylised rocks and foreground have been covered with a cobalt wash. The scene is framed in scrolled stringing. The border repeats the peony motif and there is a band of small hexagonal panels close to the rim. The rim has been painted with overglaze ochre enamel.
Impressed mark: SWANSEA
Diam 24.6cm (9.7in). Shallow foot rim. Rippled greenish-blue glaze.

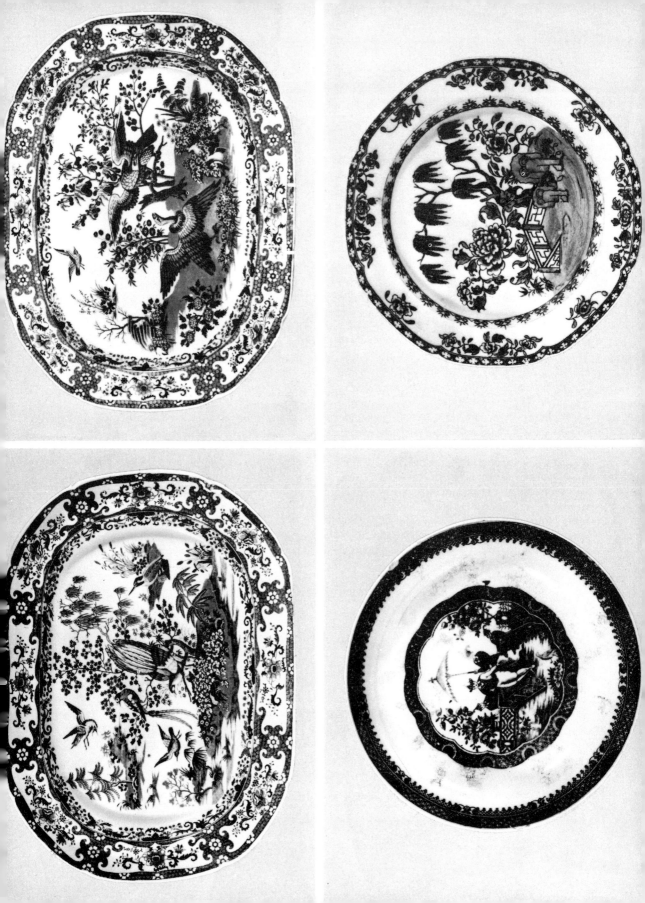

1764-1810 in the Transactions of the English Ceramic Circle Vol 7. Part 1. 1968. This is most helpful in attributing unmarked wares.

The *Chinese Scene after Pillement* (110) was taken from an illustration in *The Ladies' Amusement* (2nd edition, plate 50) and there is a Swansea jug with this design printed in underglaze black in the Glyn Vivian Art Gallery, Swansea.

The *Elephant Pattern* (111) derives its name from the resemblance of the rocks to the rear view of these quadrupeds. Grant-Davidson states that it was produced over a considerable period since it is known with early impressed marks and also with marks used after 1810. Occasionally it is found as an outline transfer but has usually been filled in with cobalt as in the example illustrated here.

The sauceboat (112) and coffee pot (113) have been attributed to Swansea for the following reasons. Firstly the printed design which has been named the *Chinoiserie Palm Pattern* occurs on a saucer in the Royal Institute of South Wales on which the word UNITY is printed on an oval reserve (*ibid.* page 70, plate 79). According to W. J. Grant-Davidson, this was the title of a Newquay pilchard-fishing company for which the Cambrian Pottery made wares. The coffee pot has two features very typical of early Swansea earthenwares—the addition of ochre to the rim and concentric raised circles on the base. The moulded spout is much larger than the orifice over which it has been placed and the inner edges of this orifice are rough. These coffee pots normally have high domed covers in which the steam hole also has a rough edge inside.

The *Cambrian Chinoiserie Ruins Pattern* (114) has many features in common with a patterns by John Davenport (Coysh, plate 26) and by the Castleford Pottery (16). These factories either used the same source or copied in part one from another.

The Turner Factory at Lane End

The *Daffodil Pattern* (115) and the *Turner Elephant Pattern* (116) are early blue-printed wares from this factory, a good deal earlier than the *Floral Pattern* and *The Village Pattern* (Coysh, plates 130-1) which were previously given too early a date and were made, in fact, *after* the bankruptcy of the Turner Brothers in 1806. The name TURNER was impressed on wares from the factory until its final closure in 1829.

The early and late wares are not difficult to distinguish. Early wares are printed in a much

112 (above left) Attributed to Cambrian Pottery, Swansea   Chinoiserie Palm Pattern (A)
Sauce boat (c 1800-1810), in dark blue, with three-storey pagoda behind a fence. Several types of tree include a prominent palm tree with fruit. A man rows on a stretch of water in a partly covered boat. A figure with the parasol stands nearby. The border inside the sauce boat is of geometrical motifs and scrolls.
Unmarked.
Length 15.5cm (6.1in). Height to top of handle 7.3cm (2.9in). Flattened foot rim. Greenish blue glaze.

113 (above right) Attributed to Cambrian Pottery, Swansea   Chinoiserie Palm Pattern (A)
Pear-shaped coffee pot (c 1800-1810) with splayed base, printed in dark blue with a scene with pagodas. Several types of tree include prominent palm trees with fruit. A man rows on a stretch of water in a partly covered boat. A figure with parasol stands on the shore. The border is of geometrical motifs and stylised sprays of flowers and leaves. Sprays with a single flower and leaves decorate the spout above and below. The rim has been painted with overglaze ochre enamel.
Height to rim 19.4cm (7.6in). Diam of base 10cm (3.9in). The foot rim slopes inward at an angle of about 45° towards two raised concentric circles. The edges of the strainer holes inside the pot have rough edges. Slightly rippled blue glaze.

114 (below left Cambrian Pottery, Swansea
Chinoiserie Ruins Pattern (A)
(Courtesy: Mr and Mrs D. A. Dalzell-Piper)
Indented plate (c 1811-17), in dark-medium blue, with a chinoiserie pattern with tropical trees and a ruined tower, partly overgrown. Two figures, by a stretch of water, one with a parasol, the other a fishing rod and line. The border of tropical trees and leaves occupies only three-quarters of the rim, leaving an unprinted area framing the central picture.
Impressed mark: DILLWYN & CO.
Diam 24.6cm (9.7in). Shallow foot rim. Almost colourless strongly rippled glaze.

115 (below right) John Turner   Daffodil Pattern (A)
Plate (c 1810-15), in dark blue, printed with sprays of flowers with daffodils on the border. Around the rim is a continuous blue band with a dentil motif.
Impressed mark: TURNER
Diam 21cm (8.3in). Shallow flattened foot rim. Rippled blue glaze on cream-coloured body.

darker blue and line engraving predominates. The later wares are printed in a lighter blue and stipple predominates. *The Turner Daffodil Pattern* (115) is very like the *Spode Gloucester Pattern* (Whiter, plate 40) and the borders are identical.

It is worth noting that Turner's *Villager Pattern* (Coysh, plate 131) was also used by Charles Heathcote & Co (1818-24). Marked pieces have been noted with almost identical moulding and only minor variations in the print.

Joseph Twigg of Newhill Pottery

According to Jewitt, Joseph Twigg was manager of the Swinton Old Pottery owned by the Bramelds until 1822 when he set up on his own and established the Newhill Pottery near Wath upon Dearne in Yorkshire. In 1833 he was joined by his brothers and the firm became Joseph Twigg & Bros until 1855, and subsequently Twigg Bros Wares from this factory are rather heavily potted and bear the impressed mark TWIGG NEWHILL in two lines. A number of patterns were used from the well-known Don Pottery series of *Named Italian Views* (Coysh, plates 36-7) but the 'name' does not always appear and the printing is seldom crisp (117). The copper plates used were obviously worn and it is possible that these were purchased from the Don Pottery when it changed ownership in 1834.

Joseph Twigg & Bros of Kilnhurst Old Pottery

In 1839 the partnership which was running the Newhill Pottery added the Kilnhurst or Thryber Dale Pottery to its interests. Wares from this factory are simply impressed TWIGG or TWIGG'S sometimes enclosed in an oval line or wreath. Rarely the letters K.P. are also included (GM3912). The TWIGG mark may, of course, have been used also at the Newhill Pottery. The *Oddfellows* plate (118) was probably made at Kilnhurst though it could have been made at Newhill for the Independent Order of Oddfellows was founded in Manchester c 1813 and had soon established lodges throughout Britain and America.

It is worth noting that the impressed TWIGG mark appears on pieces with the *Wild Rose Pattern* (Coysh, p 48) and the *Eton College Pattern* (69).

116 (*above*) *John Turner*   Animal Series (A)
                                      Elephant Pattern (A)
(*Courtesy: Mr and Mrs Martin Pulver*).
Oval dish (c 1800), in dark blue, with chinoiserie scene with pagoda and footbridge. A man with an open parasol rides an elephant with a twisted trunk. The picture is framed by a cellular band and the separate dagger border is broken by eight large insects.
Impressed mark: TURNER *beneath the Prince of Wales' feathers (GM3898).*
Length 50.8cm (20in). Width 37.1cm (114.6in). No foot rim. Almost smooth, pale greenish-blue glaze with a few 'bubbles' on base.

117 (*below left*) *Joseph Twigg*   Italian Views Series
                                     'Temple of Serapis'
(*Courtesy: Mr and Mrs Martin Pulver*)
Slightly indented plate (c 1834-40), in medium blue, with a classical scene in which three women look into the distance in the direction in which a fourth figure is pointing. They rest on a patio backed by three large columns. The border is mainly of flowers against a stipple ground with leaves. It includes an urn and two putti with sprays of flowers and descends to the well of the plate.
Impressed mark: TWIGG
                     NEWHILL
Diam 24cm (9.45in). Rounded foot rim. Rippled blue glaze. Heavy pearlware body weighing over 1lb 1oz.

118 (*below right*) *Joseph Twigg & Bros.*
                                   Oddfellows Pattern (A)
(*Courtesy: B. G. Gough, Esq*)
Plate (c 1840), in medium blue, with a pattern symbolic of the Independent Order of Oddfellows. The border is of fruit and leaves extending towards the centre of the plate from a chevron band around the rim.
Impressed mark: TWIGG *within an oval wreath.*
Diam 25.2cm (9.9in). Shallow foot rim. Smooth pale blue glaze.

Wedgwood of Etruria

Blue printing started at the Wedgwood works at Etruria in 1805 when John Wedgwood (1766-1844) was in charge of production and in the following year some patterns in the Chinese taste were exported to Russia. Very soon, however, an entirely new kind of printed decoration appeared on the Wedgwood wares. The patterns were based on some of the fine flower prints in botanical publications such as the *Botanists' Repository* (H.C. Andrews), *Paradisus Londinensis* (R. Salisbury) and the *Botanical Magazine* (William Curtis). These patterns reflected the interest of John Wedgwood who was a keen horticulturist. He had carried out many experiments in his gardens at Westbury-on-Trym near Bristol, and in 1794 had been elected a member of the Linnean Society. In 1801 he initiated discussions with eminent gardeners and as a result a meeting was held in 1804 under his chairmanship which led to the foundation of the Royal Horticultural Society. It was therefore natural that he should consider adapting some of the flower prints that interested him so much for use on blue-printed wares. Much invaluable information about the introduction of these designs was revealed in a scholarly paper read by Mrs Una des Fontaines to the Wedgwood Society in 1965 and later published in *The Proceedings of the Wedgwood Society* (No. 6. 1966. pp 69-90). With her kind permission it has been possible to include much information from this paper in the following account of these wares. The blue-printed patterns were introduced in the following sequence:

1807 *The Hibiscus Pattern* (Coysh, plate 132). The Chinese influence persists in the border of this design which has panels with oriental towers.

1807 *The Peony Pattern* (122) which has been described as 'probably one of the finest symmetrical flower patterns ever designed'. (The Prince of Wales ordered a dinner service for twelve in this pattern, with gilt, in September 1807.)

1810 *The Botanical Flowers Series* (120 and 121) of patterns which were all accurate copies of contemporary botanical prints.

1811 *The Water Lily Pattern* (119) which had been produced in brown in 1808.

The *Botanical Flowers* patterns were transferred to the wares either singly or in pairs. Numbers were engraved near the base of the stalks by which the names of the plants could be identified. So far

119 Wedgwood   'Water Lily Pattern'
Oval comport (c 1811-25) seen from above, with a pattern of water-lily and lotus flowers printed in medium blue. Inside the rim and on the handles is a 'cut-reed' border. The rim and handles are gilded. The stem of the comport (below) has a border of leaves floating in water and this is also edged with the 'cut-reed' motif.
Impressed mark: WEDGWOOD *and* G.
Length (including handles) 29.7cm (11.7in). Width 18.3cm (7.2in). Height 14cm (5.5in). No foot rim. Hollow stem. Smooth colourless glaze on white body.

as can be ascertained, no check list now exists of these engravings. There is a fine opportunity here for a purposeful collector with an interest in botany who would be prepared to compile a list of prints and trace the sources. A few have already been illustrated. No. 19, for example, appears in Mrs Una des Fontaines paper (*ibid.* Fig 5) and has been identified as *Hibiscus liliaefolius* copied from *Paradisus Londinensis* 1805-8, plate 94. Nos. 13, 20 and 23 appear here (120 and 121). A saucer in the Victoria and Albert Museum carries prints No. 36 and 39. There may well have been more than 39 in all, but this is the highest number so far noted. Two different borders or edges were used for this series. Some wares carry an edging of interlacing rings (121), others carry a bead edging (120).

The *Water Lily Pattern* (119) has an interesting history. It was 'the first Wedgwood pattern which reproduced identifiable botanical prints. What at first glance appears to be a single plant, is in fact a composition of three different plants, each with its correct leaves, flowers and fruit. The three plants are members of the family *Nymphaeaceae*, so named because they are found growing in watery places . . . Wedgwood's design depicts two genera: the genus *Nymphaea* and the genus *Nelumbium*, the actual species being *Nymphaea stellata*, *Nymphaea lotus* and *Nelumbium nucifera*. This latter specific name makes reference to the formation of the fruit or seed pod which is comparable to a nut containing kernels, that rattle in the wind'. The popular names for these three plants are the Starry water lily (on the left of the design), the Sacred Lotus of Buddha (the central flower) and the Lotus of Egypt (the two flowers on the right). The Starry water lily was derived from the *Botanists Repository* of Oct. 1803, plate 330: the Sacred Lotus of Buddha from the *Botanical Magazine* of Feb. 1806, plate 903 and the Lotus of Egypt from two distinct sources— the *Botanists Repository* of September 1804 (the half-closed flower) and the *Botanical Magazine* of Dec. 1804 (the open flower). It was undoubtedly a botanist who drew the preliminary sketch and supplied the engraver with instructions and the botanical prints to be copied. Mrs Una des Fontaines expresses her 'considered opinion that the originator and designer of the Wedgwood "Water Lily" pattern was John Wedgwood, F.H.S., F.L.S.'.

This piece of research is described in some detail to illustrate the interest that can be derived from the careful study of printed patterns.

The *Blue Claude Pattern* (124) was referred to at one time as the *Corinthian Temples* pattern. J. K.

120 (*left*) Wedgwood
     Botanical Flowers Series No. 20
(*Courtesy: Mr and Mrs J. K. des Fontaines*)
Dessert dish (c 1820-25) printed in medium blue with a flower design. The dish carries a narrow bead edging. Impressed mark: WEDGWOOD (*in small lettering*). *Length 25.4cm (10in). Foot rim. Bluish glaze.*
121 (*right*) Wedgwood
     Botanical Flowers Series Nos. 13 and 23
(*Courtesy: Robin Gurnett, Esq*)
Plate (c 1810-20), in medium blue, with two flower designs and a border of interlacing rings. Impressed mark: WEDGWOOD
Printed mark: circle and arrow (sign of Mars). Diam 24.3cm (9.7in). No foot rim. Clear and slightly rippled glaze on cream-coloured body.

des Fontaines discussed the origin and dating of this pattern in a paper read to the Wedgwood Society in 1960. (See *Proc. of the Wedgwood Soc.* No. 4. 1961 p 230). He pointed out that no reference to this design was to be found in the Wedgwood Archives and clearly regretted the confusion that might arise between 'Corinthian Temples' and 'Corinth', an alternative title for the Absalom's Pillar Pattern (Coysh, plate 137). In a paper in the *Transactions of the English Ceramic Journal* (Vol 7. Part 2. 1969 p 130) he uses the name 'Blue Claude' pointing out that the pattern has obviously been derived from a painting by Claude Lorraine. The example illustrated in his paper has the printed mark WEDGWOOD'S STONE CHINA which suggests a date early in the 1820s. The pearl-ware example (124) is from a dinner service in which all the pieces carry the same design.

The Crane Pattern (123), a title used in the *Transactions of the Eleventh Wedgwood International Seminary in Dearborn, Michigan*, in 1966, would seem to date from about the same period as the landscapes with *Blue Rose* border (Coysh, plate 136). These all make extensive use of stipple engraving. The Crane Pattern was probably introduced between 1825 and 1835.

It is interesting to note that the engravers of a number of Wedgwood patterns are known though more than one engraver was usually involved in preparing the copper-plates needed for printing a whole dinner service. These engravers include: William Brookes, a well-known designer and engraver credited with initiating the use of floral borders taken from wallpapers. He engraved Wedgwood's *Blue Bamboo* (possibly Coysh, plate 134).

William Hales also engraved the Blue Bamboo as well as the *Hibiscus Pattern* (Coysh, plate 132) and the *Peony Pattern* (122).

John Mollart engraved the *Blue Bamboo*.

John Robinson engraved the plates for the blue version of the *Water Lily Pattern* with cut-reed border (119) and some *Botanical Flowers Patterns* (120-1).

Thomas Sparkes engraved the *Hibiscus* and *Peony Patterns*. Some insight into the work of engravers is given in a paper by J. K. des Fontaines—'Letters from Thomas Sparkes, Engraver, to Wedgwood, 1815-1819', *Proc. of the Wedgwood Society*. No. 6. 1966. pp 96-100.

122 (*above left*) Wedgwood   *'Peony Pattern'*
Dished plate (c 1807), in medium and dark blue, with a pattern of peony flowers and leaves repeated four times, once in each quadrant. The border round the edge of the rim has a motif in which three small circles are grouped together. The motif is repeated on a continuous line-engraved ground.
Impressed mark: WEDGWOOD
Printed mark: B
Diam 25.1cm (9.9in). No foot rim. Slightly rippled colourless glaze on white body.

123 (*above right*) Wedgwood   *'Crane Pattern'*
Plate (c 1825-35), in medium and dark blue, with a scene in which two cranes are seen in shallow water against a background of mountains. This is almost framed in flowers and leaves. On the largest group of flowers which includes honeysuckle is a swallow-tail butterfly. The border of flowers, fruit and perched birds has a continuous background of cusped gothic arches.
Impressed marks: WEDGWOOD *and* RR
Printed mark: B
Diam 23.2cm (9.1in). No foot rim. Slightly rippled pale blue glaze.

124 (*below*) Wedgwood   *'Blue Claude Pattern'*
(*Courtesy: Mrs W. E. Haighton*)
Indented dish (c 1822) in medium and dark blue with a view of a harbour with classical buildings in the style of Claude Lorraine. The view is framed in chevron stringing and line engraving predominates. A border of leaves and flowers descends to the well of the dish. Near the rim the border pattern has a ground of S-scrolls and stylised leaves.
Impressed marks: WEDGWOOD *and* GG
Printed mark: B
Length 47cm (18.5in). Width 35.3cm (13.9in). No foot rim. Pale greenish-blue rippled glaze.

Wedgwood Marks

Most of the wares of the famous firm of Josiah Wedgwood are clearly impressed WEDGWOOD, a mark often found near the edge of the base of a plate or dish. Early pieces often have a pair of letters e.g. GG or HH impressed near the mark and although little is known about these, they do suggest a true Wedgwood origin. There are, however, a number of marks which may well confuse the inexperienced collector. These are:

1. WEDGWOOD & CO. used on early wares made at the Knottingley Pottery in Yorkshire from 1796 until 1801. They were perfectly entitled to do this since Ralph Wedgwood, a nephew of Josiah Wedgwood was a partner in the firm. The patterns, however, were printed before the Etruria factory introduced blue-printing. (pp 32-3).

2. WEDGWOOD or WEDGEWOOD was impressed on the wares of William Smith & Co of Stockton prior to 1848. In that year Messrs. Wedgwood of Etruria were granted an injunction which restrained the firm from using the name. Smith usually impressed his own mark as well (pp. 68-9).

3. WEDGWOOD & CO. was used on wares made after 1860 by Wedgwood & Co at the Unicorn and Pinnox Works, Tunstall. This impressed mark usually occurs on a heavy body together with a printed mark giving the name of the pattern (126).

4. J. WEDGWOOD sometimes occurs in marks which bear a pattern title. This was the mark of John Wedge Wood who omitted the 'e' in his second Christian name and combined it with his surname.

5. WEDGWOOD, printed as what appears to be a genuine mark, sometimes occurs on wares which are otherwise suspect. The plate with the *Blue Rose* border (125) bears no comparison in quality of body, printing or glaze, with genuine early Wedgwood pieces. It was probably made by Podmore, Walker & Wedgwood who sometimes used this mark between 1834 and 1859.

Enoch Wood & Sons of Burslem

This firm potted in Burslem between 1818 and 1846. They appear to have produced very few designs in the Chinese taste. The design with the dagger border (127), beautifully printed in dark blue, is obviously derived from the same source as the *Spode Queen Charlotte Pattern* (84).

The plate (128) with the view of *Cave Castle* is typical of the wares this firm exported to America where over 80 such British views have been recorded, most of them bearing the same grapevine border.

125 (*above left*) Possibly Podmore, Walker & Wedgwood   *'Blue Rose' style Pattern*
(*Courtesy: Mrs R. Holloway*)
Dished plate (c 1850-59), in dark-medium blue, with a river scene with sailing ship and angler. A blue rose border descends to the well of the plate.
Impressed mark: WEDGWOOD *and* 3
Diam 21.6 (8.5in). No foot rim. Smooth colourless glaze.

126 (*above right*) Wedgwood & Co.
         'Corinthia' Pattern
Dished plate (c 1860), in medium blue, with an Italian scene. The border has a stipple ground with scrolled medallions, each with an Italian scene.
Impressed mark: WEDGWOOD & CO.
Printed mark: CORINTHIA *in a scrolled panel with the marker's name below—WEDGWOOD & CO.*
Diam 21.2cm (8.4in). Smooth colourless glaze on heavy ironstone body. Weight nearly 1lb.

127 (*below left*) Enoch Wood & Sons
       Dagger-border Chinoiserie (A)
Indented plate (c 1818-30), in dark blue, with a Chinese scene with pagodas and a single-arch bridge. Two figures on and near the bridge face the main pagoda. The picture is framed in a cellular band. The border consists of a dark blue outer band and an inner 'dagger' band.
Impressed mark: ENOCH WOOD & SONS *printed around an eagle with the word* BURSLEM *beneath.*

128 (*below right*) Enoch Wood & Sons.
       English Views Series
       'Cave Castle, Yorkshire'
(*Courtesy: Ian Henderson, Esq*)
Indented plate (c 1818-30) in dark blue, with a view of Cave Castle, Yorkshire from the parkland in which there are cows at pasture. A boat sails on the park lake. The wide border of grapes, vine leaves and convolvulus flowers has a cellular ground and descends to the well of the plate.
Impressed mark: ENOCH WOOD & SONS *printed around an eagle with the word* BURSLEM *beneath (GM4257).*
Printed mark: CAVE CASTLE YORKSHIRE *on a ribbon with flowers and leaves.*
Diam 21.3cm (8.4in). Double foot rim. Slightly rippled greenish-blue glaze.

Problem Pieces

Some Puzzling Marks

The *Cuba Pattern* plate (129) was probably made in Staffordshire for export to Cuba and is printed in the dark blue so much favoured in America between about 1820 and 1840. It seems to have been part of a special order for a coffee house supplied through the wholesale importers—the ALMACAN DE GAMBAY Co of Havana. The pattern is a tribute of love to the beautiful girls of Cuba and the lines below the map tell us that when Paris had to choose 'the fairest' among Venus, Juno and Pallas he eventually took a Cuban girl brought by Cupid saying that she was the fairest of them all. Who made this export piece? It could well have been any of four or five firms—Adams, Clews, Hall, Ralph Stevenson or Enoch Wood. The layout and lettering are very similar to that on an America and Independence States Plate made by James and Ralph Clews. Similar stringing round the rim was used by Ralph Stevenson on a plate showing the State House, Hartford. On the other hand, it is known that Thomas Adams, the younger brother of William Adams of Stoke, opened premises in Mexico early in the 1830s from which he built up a connection with Cuba and Brazil.

The *Grecian Statue* plate (130) bears the initials W. & B. which probably stand for Wood and Brownfield of Cobridge (1838-50) but could possibly stand for Wood and Bowers of Burslem (c 1839).

The *Sun and Fountain Pattern* (131) has a good clear mark but this is not a maker's mark. J. Green & Sons is the name of a London retail firm which had premises at 10 and 11 St. Paul's Churchyard from 1841-2. Prior to that date the firm had been known as J. Green & Co (GM page 288).

The *Two-man Scroll Pattern* (132) marked HILCOCK in letters 0.5cm high bears a remarkable similarity to Swansea and Leeds patterns produced c 1800 (Coysh, plates 10 and 12). There are, however, significant differences in the pattern and particularly in the potting. The diameter of this plate is slightly smaller, the rippled glaze is bluer than any noted elsewhere on wares of the period and there is no foot rim whereas both the Swansea and Leeds examples carry foot rims. No potter of the name can be traced, nor does it seem likely at this early period that it is the mark of a retailer, though a firm called Hillcock & Walton must have existed at a latter date either as potters or retailers (Little, p 73).

129 (above left) Possibly W. Adams of Stoke
Cuba Pattern (A)
Slightly indented dished plate (c 1820-30), in very dark blue, with a map of Cuba surmounted by a cupid and the words AL AMOR DE LAS BILLISIMAS. *On either side is a fluted column and below a verse in Spanish. The wide border of flowers and fruit merges with the central design.*
Printed mark: LA CAFETERA
      ALMACEN DE GAMBAY CO.
      HAVANA
Diam 22.6cm (8.9in). Double foot rim. Slightly rippled blue glaze.

130 (above right) Probably Wood & Brownfield
'Grecian Statue' Pattern
Plate (c 1838) with wavy edge, in light and medium blue, with a Grecian scene in which a statue of a woman on horseback is a central figure. A wide border with vases of flowers on a stipple ground is broken by floral medallions with architectural motifs.
Printed mark: A panel with the words
      GRECIAN STATUE
      STONE-WARE
surmounted by the pre-1837 Royal Arms with inescutcheon. Below are the letters W. & B.
Diam 27cm (10.6in). Rounded foot rim. Smooth colourless glaze.

131 (below left) Unknown maker
Sun and Fountain Pattern (A)
Indented dished plate (c 1840-2), in medium and dark blue, with a scene of a large fountain gushing water. The border which descends to the well of the plate is of flowers against a stipple ground.
Impressed mark: J. Green & Sons
Diam 25.2cm (9.9in). Double foot rim. Slightly rippled pale blue glaze.

132 (below right) Unknown maker
Two man/scroll Pattern (A)
Indented plate (c 1800) with chinoiserie pattern in dark-medium blue. Two pagodas are linked by a three-arch bridge on which there are two small figures. The picture is framed in a band of geometrical motifs broken in four places by stylised flowers. The border is of geometrical motifs, scrolls, flowers and Chinese writing scrolls.
Impressed mark: HILCOCK *in very large capitals.*
Diam 24cm (9.5in). No foot rim. Rippled blue glaze.

Named Views

A remarkably large number of blue-printed topographical scenes bear the name of a place but no maker's name. Indeed, these are frequently sought after by collectors because they often have interesting associations or reveal facts about buildings that have disappeared or have changed beyond recognition.

At first sight the plate and mug (133a and b) with the *View of Leighton Buzzard Church* would seem to carry a maker's name but the only firm with the name of Neale existing after 1786 was Neale & Bailey of Church Works, Hanley (sometimes Neale & Co) which operated from 1790-1814 and had premises at 8, St. Paul's Churchyard. The plate and mug (133a and 133b) appear to be later. Enquiries led to the discovery that *Pigot's Commercial Directory* for 1823-4 lists Nathaniel Neal of the High Street, Leighton Buzzard as a glass and china dealer. In the 1830-1 edition the name is spelt Neale (possibly a correction of an earlier mis-spelling). It is also reported that there are people in the town who have similar examples showing a print of the Market Cross. It could well be that Nathaniel Neale of Leighton Buzzard had some connections in Staffordshire (or was a retired potter himself) who decided to embark on a local commercial venture. Only one engraving of the church was made: the print on the mug is the same print with some foreground removed and the border pattern has had to be cut away to make room for the spire. These pieces have been labelled as 'possibly Enoch Wood & Sons' since the colour corresponds to that on his export wares and the 'Wild Rose' border (later used by many other potters) was printed by his firm with architectural subjects such as the Boston State House.

Many series of topographical views carry a series title e.g. *Antique Scenery, English Scenery* (Coysh, plate 157) and *Metropolitan Scenery* without a maker's name, but with the name of a particular scene. The *Antique Scenery* view of *Hexham Abbey* (134) is a good example. Clues are badly needed which will lead to the identification of the makers of these series but nevertheless these scenes have an inherent interest.

The titles of the scenes of *Monmouth* (136) and *The Powder Mill, Hastings* (135) are enclosed in an eight-sided panel made of tiny touching circles. A similar panel has been noted on wares of a later date by F. & R. Pratt of Fenton. It contains the words—PRATT'S NATIVE SCENERY. This is a

133a (above left) Possibly Enoch Wood & Sons
Leighton Buzzard Church
(Courtesy: Robin Gurnett, Esq)
Plate (c 1825-30), in dark blue, with 'A north-west view of Leighton Buzzard Church' printed beneath a view of the spired church in the well of the plate. A narrow border of the 'Wild Rose' pattern is printed around the dished rim.
Printed mark: N. NEALE
Diam 25.8cm (10.15in). Double foot rim. Blue glaze on cream coloured body.

133b (above right) Possibly Enoch Wood & Sons
Leighton Buzzard Church
(Courtesy: Ian Henderson, Esq)
Mug (c 1825-30) with straight sides, and a ribbed band around the base with the pattern and border as on 133a. Handle with acanthus-style moulded ends.
Printed mark: A NORTH-WEST VIEW OF LEIGHTON BUZZARD CHURCH N. NEALE
Height 12.1cm (4.8in). Diam of base 9.3cm (3.7in). Blue glaze on cream-coloured body.

134 (below left) Unknown maker
'Antique Scenery' Series
Hexham Abbey
(Courtesy: Richard Clements, Esq)
Indented plate (c 1820-40), in medium blue, with a view of Hexham Abbey. The border of scrolls and flowers on a lattice ground descends to the well of the plate.
Printed mark: HEXHAM ABBEY *within a cartouche bearing the series title* ANTIQUE SCENERY, *the whole surmounted by a crown.*
Diam 21.4cm (8.3in). Double foot rim. Smooth pale blue glaze.

135 (below right) Possibly F. & R. Pratt & Co
Powder Mill, Hastings
Dished indented plate (c 1820-40) with a view of Powder Mill, Hastings. The scene is framed in bands of blue and white and the border of flowers (mainly roses) descends towards the well of the plate. The outer part of the border has a stipple ground; the inner part has a cross-hatched line-engraved ground. The flowers have been decorated over the glaze with pink, green and yellow enamels. The edge of the rim is gilded.
Printed mark: Powder Mill, Hastings, *near the rim of the plate within an eight-sided panel bounded by small circles.*
Diam 24.6cm (9.7in). Narrow double foot rim. Rippled blue glaze.

pattern earlier used by Adams (Coysh, plate 17). F. & R. Pratt operated from 1818 and became experienced transfer-printers. No early blue-printed wares have been noted, however, with the name or initials of this firm. It is just possible that these named views (135 and 136) were made by Pratt but the evidence is slender. The *Powder Mill* example (135) is interesting because the printed border has been painted over in places with coloured enamels; such examples are not uncommon in this series. Other localities illustrated on wares with the same border and similar mark are: Bysham Monastery, Kirkham Abbey, Netley Abbey, Linlithgow Palace, and Thorpe in Derbyshire.

A large dish (137) by an unknown maker is of particular interest because it has been possible to identify the scene. The view is of Lee in Kent. It is taken from Angus's *Select Views of Seats*, Plate XLIII, from an engraving dated 1796, after Claude Nattes. (Lee is on the River Lea in the Borough of Lewisham, 1½ miles south-east of Greenwich.)

A series of topographical scenes which all carry similar borders present an interesting problem. Some are unmarked, some bear a printed 'rock cartouche' with the name of the view (138), and some are impressed ROGERS but do not name the scene (139 and Coysh, plate 89). They are not uncommon, particularly the named views which are known to include Byland Abbey, Jedburgh, and Sweetheart Abbey (138) in Kircudbrightshire which was where William Paterson (1658-1719), founder of the Bank of England, spent the last years of his life. Why should the examples with the printed title have no maker's name? A collector has recently reported a dish with a border identical with that of 138 impressed DILLWYN.

136 (*above left*) *Possibly F. & R. Pratt*
Monmouth
Indented tureen stand (c 1820-40), in medium blue, with a central view of Monmouth with stone houses and cattle in the foreground. The scene is framed in a printed border as in 135.
Printed mark: Monmouth *in an eight-sided panel bounded by small circles.*
Length 36.1cm (14.2in). Width 27.9cm (11.0in). Recessed base. Slightly rippled pale blue glaze.

137 (*above right*) *Maker unknown* Lee, Kent (A)
(*Courtesy: Mrs Elizabeth Carter*)
Indented and cusped dish (c 1820), in medium blue, with a view of Lee, Kent, seen looking across a lake with swans. The border has four medallions, each with a different country scene, separated by sprays of large flowers. The central picture is framed and the rim of the dish carries a band of geometrical motifs.
Unmarked.
Length 48.3cm (19in). Width 41.9cm (16.5in). Three curved gravy channels run into a central channel which ends in a gray well. At the opposite end of the two sides are ogee rims which raise the dish. Rippled blue glaze.

138 (*below left*) *Possibly Dillwyn of Swansea*
Sweetheart Abbey
Eight-sided dish (c 1824-36), double-printed in medium and dark blue with a view of Sweetheart Abbey. The large flowers of the border descend from the stipple ground of the rim towards the well of the dish.
Printed mark: SWEETHEART ABBEY *on a rock cartouche.*
Length 42.4cm (16.7in). Width 32.5cm (12.8in).

139 (*below right*) *John Rogers & Son*
View of Durham (A)
(*Courtesy: Mrs V. Heap*)
Eight-sided dish (c 1814-36) in medium blue, with a view of Durham Cathedral. The large flowers of the border descend from the stipple ground of the rim towards the well of the dish.
Impressed mark: ROGERS
Length 47.7cm (18.8in). Width 36.1cm (14.2in). No foot rim. Rippled blue glaze.

Unmarked Wares

Many collectors avoid unmarked pieces but these are often worth buying if they are of good quality not only for their decorative value but for the interest derived from the attempt to solve some of the problems they present.

The Indian Procession (140) bears certain similarities to both Rogers wares and Herculaneum wares. The scene is very similar to those in Thomas Daniell's *Oriental Scenery*. The general character of the body, glaze, etc, is very like that from the Liverpool Herculaneum factory (compare 140 with 42 and 43).

The Bridge Pattern (141) is printed in a dark blue colour very similar to that used by Ralph Hall on his export wares (Coysh, plates 45 and 46) and marked examples of his wares are known to have included the chain-link motif. However, the potting is heavier than is normal with Ralph Hall pieces.

The bordaloue (142) with the *Castle Gateway Pattern* has a design which is very difficult to attribute. The Liverpool Herculaneum Pottery, however, made considerable use of scrolled medallions in the 1820-30 period (see Smith, A. *The Illustrated Guide to Liverpool Herculaneum Pottery*, plates 162, 165 and 166A); moreover, the flared shape also suggests a comparison with Herculaneum wares (*ibid.* plate 149).

The invalid feeding cup (143) has a pattern in the style of the Spode *Blue Rose Pattern* (Whiter plate 55) and the potting suggests the 1835-50 period. Spode, Copeland & Garrett, Davenport and Rogers are all known to have made feeding cups before 1850 but Davenport and Rogers were not given to the use of floral patterns. This field of medical ceramics is an interesting and specialized one. Those interested are urged to visit the Wellcome Institute of the History of Medicine in the Euston Road, London N.W.1. It is normally open to the public on weekdays (except Bank Holiday weekends).

140 (above left) Possibly Herculaneum
Indian Procession Pattern (A)
Indented dish (c 1810-20), in medium to dark blue, with an Indian scene with large domed building. In the foreground is a procession in which an elephant with howdah is preceded by two horsemen and a group of men on foot carrying shields and lances or flags. The border merges with the central scene.
Unmarked.
Length 38.6cm (15.2in). Width 31cm (12.2in). No Foot rim. Rippled pale blue glaze.

141 (above right) Possibly Ralph Hall
Bridge Pattern (A)
Indented dish (c 1820-30), in dark blue, with a river scene with bridge and buildings. There are two figures in the foreground and two men in a boat on the river. The picture is framed in stringing and the border, which descends to the well of the dish, is of flower and leaf-scrolls. There is a chain-link motif round the rim.
Unmarked.
Length 32.5cm (12.8in). Width 30cm (11.8in). No foot rim. Base combed. Smooth colourless glaze.

142 (below left) Possibly Herculaneum
Castle Gateway Pattern (A)
Moulded bourdaloue (c 1820-30), in medium blue, with a floral background and border on a stipple ground with large scrolled medallions with a view of a castle gateway.
Unmarked.
Length (including handle) 24.38cm (9.6in). The bordaloue is waisted and slightly flared at the rim.

143 (below right) Possibly Copeland & Garrett
Rose Pattern (A)
(Courtesy: The Wellcome Trustees)
Invalid feeding cup (c 1840), in medium blue, with a Blue Rose-style pattern of wild roses and other flowers with foliage. The top is partly covered.
Printed mark: F
Length 11.9cm (4.7in). Width 7.2cm (2.8in). Prominent foot rim. Smooth colourless glaze.

The *Classical Ruins Pattern* (144) is usually attributed to Thomas Lakin of Stoke on the grounds that there is said to be a single plate with this pattern impressed 'Lakin' in lower-case letters in the Victoria and Albert Museum. Williams (p 240) states that 'it seems probable that the Pyramid in the picture is the Caius Cestius monument, built in Rome about 30 BC'. The unmarked example illustrated by Williams (Fig. 176) is, however, markedly different from the plate shown here (144). It has a long-horned goat to the *left* of the man and there are other variations so that it may well be that this pattern was used by more than one potter. Thomas Lakin & Son made earthenwares from 1810-1812 and continued as Thomas Lakin until 1817. The only listed mark is LAKIN impressed in capitals (GM2311).

The *Fisherman*, or *Pleasure Boat Pattern* (145) is well known on Caughley porcelain (G. A. Godden. *Collectors Guide*, October, 1967. pp 44-7). Until the white-ware plate with feather-moulded edge touched over in blue enamel was discovered, no other pottery wares had been noted by the author with this pattern. It is printed in reverse and appears to be nearer to the Caughley version than the Worcester version. The fact that it is in reverse may be due to the fact that it was copied from a print from a copperplate rather than direct from a piece of porcelain. What factory could have made this plate? A number of potters have produced white-wares of this type including Joshua Heath, Spode (Whiter, plate 104), and Swansea (Lewis, A. *Collector's History of English Pottery*, plate 212). It is, however, impossible to attribute this plate to a particular maker.

The *Cheetah Pattern* (146) on a bowl of particularly good quality provides another insoluble problem. The glaze is remarkably blue and the potting is thin. It was clearly made by one of the early factories engaged in producing blue-printed wares.

The *Giraffe and Camel Pattern* (147) is not uncommon but no marked examples have been traced. Among the potters who made octagonal plates were Joshua Heath of Hanley who ceased to operate in 1800 and Brameld (10 and 11) but these shapes were not combined with indentations.

144 (above left) Probably Thomas Lakin
'Classical Ruins' Pattern
Indented plate (1812-17), in dark blue, with a scene with classical ruins which include the statue of a recumbent man. In the foreground is a goatherd with goat beside a rapidly flowing stream. The border includes three scenes, each repeated, including a farmyard scene with cows.
Unmarked.
Diam 25.1cm (9.9in). Single foot rim. Thick blue glaze.

145 (above right) Maker unknown
'Fisherman Pattern'
Plate (c 1800) with blue-enamelled scalloped edge, printed in dark blue with a version of the fisherman pattern with five smaller riverside scenes around it.
Unmarked.
Diam 24.8cm (9.8in). No foot rim. Strongly rippled blue glaze.

146 (below left) Maker unknown
Cheetah Pattern (A)
Bowl (c 1800-1810) in dark blue, with a scene in which a cheetah is hunting an antelope. The border of stylised trees and plants is broken by scenes with domed buildings.
Unmarked.
Diam 25.9cm (10.1in). Splayed foot rim 2.1cm (0.8in). Blue rippled glaze. Three prominent stilt-marks.

147 (below right) Maker unknown
Giraffe and Camel Willow Pattern (A)
Eight-sided indented plate (c 1810-20) with a willow-pattern-style Chinese scene in which a giraffe and camel are prominent. The scene is enclosed in a band of scrolled motifs and the border is of geometrical and scrolled motifs.
Unmarked.
Diam 24.7cm (9.7in). Double foot rim. Greenish-blue rippled glaze.

Commemorative and Sporting Prints

The plate (148) with the printed mark of an igloo which includes the words ARCTIC SCENERY is obviously meant to mark a journey of Arctic exploration, possibly one undertaken by officers of the Hudson Bay Company. Among the men who were involved in such expeditions between 1800 and 1850 were:

Sir George Back (1796-1878) between 1819 and 1837

Sir John Franklin (1786-1847) between 1818 and 1847

Dr Richard King (1811-1876) between 1833 and 1850

Sir William Edward Parry (1790-1855) between 1819 and 1827

John Rae (1813-1893) between 1846 and 1855

Sir John Richardson (1787-1865) between 1825 and 1849

Sir James Clark Ross (1800-1862) between 1819 and 1831

Thomas Simpson (1808-1840) between 1836-9.

All these men wrote narratives of their journeys and somewhere among these there may be an engraving from which the pattern on this Arctic Scenery plate was derived. The scene seems most likely to represent the 1827 expedition of Sir William Parry who tried to reach the North Pole from Spitzbergen by travelling with sledge-boats over the ice and reached the highest latitude attained before 1876.

Shooting with Dogs (149) bears a close resemblance to the sporting series produced by Enoch Wood & Sons (Coysh, plates 140 and 141) but it has a different border. Perhaps the engraver of the Wood design engraved a similar set for another potter. It is a fine quality jug.

The Trafalgar Pattern (150) occurs on thinly potted tea wares which carry a red rim and bear the word TRAFALGAR. These must have been produced soon after the great victory of 1805.

The Neptune Pattern (151) is commoner than the Trafalgar Pattern but is of poorer quality. The potting is thick and the transferred design is seldom crisp. It was probably produced a good deal later as a general affirmation of the fact that Britain ruled the waves. The heads in the medallions vary slightly, but the differences would appear to be only those resulting from rather poor engraving. Williams, however, expressed the view that they are meant to represent men who were concerned with the sea victories of the time (p 243).

148 (above left) Maker unknown

'Arctic Scenery'

Dished plate (c 1840-50) with wavy edge, in medium violet-blue, with an arctic scene with two ships and a sledge with eskimos drawn by dogs. The wide border has alternate panels of flowers and tropical animals. The stipple ground descends towards the well of the plate where it has a decorative edge.

Printed mark: ARCTIC SCENERY printed on an igloo with icebergs behind. (The mark is placed near the rim of the plate).

Diam 27cm (10.7in). Double foot rim. Smooth colourless glaze.

149 (above right) Maker unknown

Shooting with Dogs (A)

Jug (c 1820-30), in medium blue, encircled by a country scene with a cottage and a horse with foal. In the centre of the scene is a marksman shooting at a bird. He has three gun dogs. The border of scrolls and flowers is printed inside and outside the jug. Unmarked.

Diam at recessed base 12cm (4.7in). Height to rim 16.7cm (6.5in). Smooth blue glaze.

150 (below left) Maker unknown

Trafalgar Pattern (A)

Teabowl (c 1805-25) in dark blue, the outside with entwined mermen blowing trumpets. Inside the cup is a border with Union Jacks, anchors and medallions and a coastal scene with palm tree. Inside the bowl, the base has a cusped medallion bearing the word TRAFALGAR on a ribbon with a Union Jack and a cannon. Unmarked.

Diam 8.7cm (3.4in). Height 5cm (1.95in). Flattened foot rim. Impressed circle in centre of base. Red enamel on rim.

151 (below right) Maker unknown

Neptune Pattern (A)

(Courtesy: Mrs D. Pugh)

Dished indented plate (c 1815-20), in medium to dark blue, with a design showing Neptune with Britannia 'ruling the waves'. A flying putti announces victories. The border, which is separated from the central design by stringing, shows groups of military accoutrements and female figures holding medallions with the heads of a victorious leader or leaders.

Diam 24.2cm (9.5in). No foot rim. Smooth colourless glaze.

Small Wares

Small plates were often made for children and carry appropriate decoration—a scene from a story such as Robinson Crusoe (152), a righteous proverb, or a country scene with children (153). They nearly always have moulded borders, sometimes with the letters of the alphabet, sometimes with moulded flowers. The daisy border (152) was popular and was used by William Smith & Co of Stockton and other makers. These plates are very seldom marked.

Miniature dinner services were made at an earlier date by a number of firms (Coysh, plate 87). The engraved patterns are often tailored to the shapes and they may be considered as traveller's samples though firms later produced such sets as 'dolly' or 'toy' services for children to play with.

American Cup Plates

In America small plates with a diameter of less than 12cm are usually described as 'cup plates'. The earliest reference the author has traced to the use of this term is a statement by Moore in 1903. 'Great-grandmama could not bear to have her linen stained, or her mahogany marred by the rims of tea cups; so when the fragrant Bohea was poured into the saucer to cool, the cup was neatly placed in the little plate provided for it.' The author has sought in vain for an earlier reference and for evidence that this method of drinking tea was common in the early nineteenth century. Cup plates are not listed in contemporary bills, accounts or inventories which list tea-wares. Indeed ,they seem to be unknown in Britain and do not appear in the records of earthenware makers. Nor do contemporary prints show cup plates (see 82). Yet in America the little plates shown here (154-5) would be described as cup plates although the plate marked CLEWS is *known to be* from a miniature dinner service. The author has been forced to the conclusion that so-called 'cup plates' are from services of this type made either as samples to show patterns or colours, or as toy services for children. The recent undated catalogue of *Historical China Cup Plates* compiled R. N. and V. A. Wood of Baltimore, Maryland, lists some 134 patterns some on plates up to 12.5cm diameter. Can any *evidence* be provided to prove that these were items in tea services imported into America? Do they have their counterparts in porcelain services? Or must one assume that earthenware cup plates are a myth?

152 (*above left*) *Possibly William Smith & Co of Stockton* 'Robinson Crusoe'
Moulded child's plate (c 1840-50) printed in medium blue with a scene from Defoe's 'Robinson Crusoe'. The border is moulded with three rows of daisies and a black line has been painted near the rim before glazing. Unmarked.
Diam 13.1cm (5.1in). Rounded foot rim. Smooth pale blue glaze on white body.

153 (*above right*) *Maker unknown*
Feeding Turkeys (A)
(*Courtesy: Mrs Jean Latham*)
Child's plate (c 1840-50), in medium blue, with a view of a woman and child feeding turkeys. The rim is ringed with black (underglaze) and the edge of the plate has gadrooned moulding. Unmarked.
Diam 12.4cm (4.9in). Rounded foot rim. Three groups of three stilt marks within the footrim. Smooth pale blue glaze.

154 (*below left*) *Maker unknown*
Picking Apples (A)
(*Courtesy: Mrs Elizabeth Carter*)
Toy plate (c 1815-25), in medium blue, with a scene showing two boys, one in an apple tree, the other on a ladder leaning against the tree. They are picking apples and dropping them into the pinafore of a girl standing below. Two baskets of apples stand on the ground. Nearby is a cottage doorway. The scene covers the whole plate except for a line of beading on the outer edge of the rim.
Impressed mark: a small six-pointed star in a circle. Diam 11.2cm (4.4in). No foot rim. Slightly rippled blue glaze.

155 (*below right*) *J. & R. Clews*
(*Courtesy: Robin Gurnett, Esq*)
Toy plate (c 1818-34), in dark blue, with fragments of scenes including a lake with two figures on one half and a lake with sailing boat on the other.
Impressed mark: CLEWS'S WARRANTED between concentric circles. Within the inner circle is a crown. Diam 9.1cm (3.05in). Double foot rim. Deep blue glaze.

INDEX

(numbers refer to pages)

Adams, Benjamin, 10, 11
Adams, William of Cobridge, 10
Adams, William of Greengates, 10, 12, 13
Adams, William of Stoke, 10, 11, 13, 98, 99
Alcock, Samuel, & Co, 56
Ashworth, G. L., 44

Bathwell & Goodfellow, 12, 13
Bentley, Wear & Bourne,
Bo'ness Pottery, 14, 15
Brameld & Co, 14-19
Brameld, John, 14
Bristol Pottery, 58-61

Cambrian Pottery, 84-87
Carey, Thomas & John, 18, 19
Castleford Pottery, 18, 19
Caughley, 106
Chesworth & Robinson, 20
Chesworth & Wood, 20
Chetham & Robinson, 20, 21
Clews, James & Ralph, 8, 10, 20, 21, 110
Copeland & Garrett, 22-3

Dalton & Burn, 26
Daniel, Walter, 22-3
Davenport, Henry & William, 24-5
Davenport, John, 24-5
Davenport, William & Co, 24-7
Deakin & Bailey, 26-7
Dillwyn & Co, 87
Dimmock, Thomas & Co, 26-7
Don Pottery, 28-31, 88
Dunderdale, David, & Co, 18, 19

Edwards, James, 56
Elkin & Co, 30, 31
Elkin, Knight & Elkin, 30
Elkin, Knight & Co, 30
Elkin, Knight & Bridgwood, 30

Fell, Thomas, & Co, 30, 31
Ferrybridge Pottery, 32-3
Foley Potteries, 30

Garrison Pottery, Sunderland, 54
Godwin, Thomas, 32-3
Godwin, Thomas & Benjamin, 32

Goodwin, Bridgwood & Orton, 34, 35
Goodwins & Harris, 34, 35
Green, J. & Co, 98
Green, J. & Sons, 98, 99
Green, John William & Co, 28
Greens, Bingley & Co, 14
Greens, Hartley & Co, 14

Hall, Ralph, 104-5
Hartley, Greens & Co, 42, 43, 54
Harvey, Charles & Sons, 34-5
Harvey, C. & W. K., 34
Heath, John, of Burslem, 36-7
Heath, Joshua, of Hanley, 106
Heathcote, Charles, & Co, 88
Henshall & Co, 12, 36-7
Henshall & Williamson, 36
Herculaneum Pottery, 36-9, 104-5
Hicks & Meigh, 38
Hicks, Meigh & Johnson, 38-41
Higginbotham, 46
Hilcock, 98, 99

Jamieson, J., & Co, 14, 15
Jones & Son of Hanley, 40, 41

Kilnhurst Old Pottery, 88
Knottingley Pottery, 32-3

Lakin, Thomas, 104-5
Leeds Old Pottery, 42-3, 54
Liverpool Herculaneum Pottery, 36-9, 104-5

Mason, C. J. & Co, 44-7
Mason, G. M. & C. J., 44-7
Mason Miles, 44
Mason, W., 44-5
May, Robert, 46-7
Meir, John, 48-9
Meir, John & Son, 50, 51
Minton, Arthur, 52
Minton, Herbert, 52
Minton, Thomas, 52
Minton & Boyle, 52-3
Minton & Co, 52-3
Moore, Samuel & Co, 54, 55
Morley, Francis & Co, 44, 54-55
Muir, James & Andrew, 84

Neale, Nathaniel, 100, 101

Newhill Pottery, 88

Pettys & Co, 42, 54-5
Petty & Hewitt, 54
Petty, Samuel & Son, 54
Phillips, Edward & George, 56-59
Phillips, George, 58-9
Podmore, Walker & Wedgwood 124-5
Poulson, Joseph, 52
Pountney & Allies, 58-61
Pratt, F. & R., & Co, 100-103

Rainforth & Co, 54
Reed, Taylor & Co, 32
Reed, Taylor & Kelsall, 32
Robinson, John, 8, 94
Ridgway, John & William, 62-3
Ridgway, Morley, Wear & Co, 64-5
Ridgway, William & Co, 62, 64-5
Riley, John & Richard, 7, 64-5
Rockingham China Works, 14
Rogers, John, & Son, 66-7, 102-3
Rogers, John & George,

Sewell of Newcastle-upon-Tyne, 68
Shirley, Thomas & Co, 84
Smith, William, & Co, 68, 69, 110
Spode, 16, 68-80
Stevenson, Andrew, 82
Stevenson, James, 84
Stevenson, Ralph, 82
Stevenson & Williams, 82
Swansea, See Cambrian Pottery
Swinton Old Pottery, 14-19, 88

Toft & May, 46
Tomlinson, William, & Co, 32
Turner, Brothers, 86-89
Turner, John, 87
Twigg, Joseph, 88, 89
Twigg, Joseph & Brothers, 88, 89

Wear Pottery, Southwick, 54
Wedgewood, 68, 69, 86
Wedgwood & Co, 86-7
Wedgwood (Etruria), 7, 8, 90-95
Wedgwood, John, 8, 90, 92
Wedgwood, Ralph, 32
Wood, Enoch & Sons, 96-7, 108
Wood, John Wedge, 96
Wood & Bowers, 98
Wood & Brownfield, 98, 99